FORUM:

The Secret Advantage of
Successful Leaders

FORUM:
The Secret Advantage of Successful Leaders

MO FATHELBAB

Contact information for Mo Fathelbab and Forum Resources Network
web: www.forumnet.net
tel: +1.703.836.7800
e-mail: maf@forumnet.net

Cover and interior design created by Karen Seidman
of Seidman Says Communications (Washington, DC)
web: www.seidmansays.biz

Cataloging in Publication Data
(Mo Fathelbab) (FORUM: The Secret Advantage of Successful Leaders)

ISBN 978-1-4303-2781-3

Manufactured in the United States of America

Thank You

Thank you to all who have contributed to this book both directly and indirectly. This book has been years in the making, and I couldn't have done it without my clients, affiliates and our excellent team of facilitators.

There are so many people to express my appreciation to, but in particular, I would like to give special mention to Jorge Cherbosque (The Castle) and Jim Kochalka (The Life Walk) for their work in creating exercises to help build relationships and trust.

Special thanks are also extended to Rachael Garrity and Jula Kinnaird for their masterful skill in text editing, as well as Karen Seidman who was responsible for designing the cover art and the layout of the book. Thank you too to Victoria Putri for her skillful photography and Dawn Espinoza as photo stylist. I'd be remiss if I also did not expressly thank my colleague Barbara Buzzell for all her hard work and support.

And thank you Verne Harnish for being the best teacher I've had and for introducing me to the Young Entrepreneurs' Organization in 1989.

As I have developed my own peer group experiences, I have been reminded again and again how important consistent support can be. For that I will be forever grateful to my mother, who has been "on my team" every day, all day.

And to Sally Hurley, my life partner, I am grateful for her patience with the risks, long hours and interminable travel that I've faced to do the work I love; and beyond that, for her ability through it all to stay who and how she is.

Mo

Table of Contents

***"Keep company with those
who may make you better."***

-English saying

Preface

Because it was designed for meetings with the firm's most prestigious clients, the room is smaller than most on the executive floor, tastefully appointed, completely private. The seven men and five women who sit around the mahogany table are, from both dress and demeanor, clearly comfortable in such an environment. The youngest, a tall, lanky athlete turned entrepreneur, is listening intently. Across the table, a dark-haired woman whose face and name are familiar to anyone interested in investment banking, is struggling for composure. While some of those in the room are leaning forward with their elbows on the table, others look at her across tented hands. Next to her an older man quietly puts his hand on her forearm in a silent, but strong, gesture of reassurance. Interestingly, there are no cell phones on the table, no PDAs, in fact, almost no paper. At least this element of the corridors of power is different today, as it is the second Monday afternoon of the month.

Meanwhile, 15 blocks away and 17 stories down, in a room that is considerably larger, lighter, and perhaps one could say more "creatively" furnished, another group is talking animatedly. Before a flipchart in the corner stands another athlete, this one female and, though she isn't happy it shows, flustered. Her fingertips are emblazoned with blue ink from the marker she's using, and the paper in front of her crackles as she continues to explain her project. Here, too, the only paper on the table is a set of notes and charts she has distributed. One man has taken off his wristwatch and positioned it on the table to make it easy to check the elapsed time. At the end of the table, a middle-aged man who could be a double for

Harrison Ford is asking a question. Everyone else in the room, save one woman who is frantically looking in her purse for the cell phone she forgot to put on vibrate, is listening intently.

Every day, every week, every month scenes like these appear throughout the Western (and parts of the Eastern) world. They involve all sorts of people, in all sorts of careers, and doing all kinds of things. What they have in common is the shared recognition that, as your mother and mine might have said, "Two heads are better than one." But more, much more. Because there are not only two heads, but a dozen or so, each choosing to be engaged because he or she knows there is common ground around which grows a wealth of ideas, experiences and approaches that may not be common at all. What these groups are called varies widely. Ones operating in the business world or the higher socioeconomic levels will often use titles such as *forum* or *roundtable*. Those created among public service organizations or for personal reasons may often be called a *group* or *club*. The name matters little. The purpose, the structure and the ways of operating matter a great deal.

By providing an honest exchange of ideas and experience, these groups give participants an opportunity to increase their success potential in all parts of their professional and personal lives. And, in most every case, the impetus is an experience completely different from any other human exchange.

Groups that work well offer their members an unequalled source of information, ideas and, when needed, support. Still, they differ distinctly from what is most normally called a "support group." The mission is one of shared experience and honesty and the environment is one of confidentiality, but these groups do not focus on people who are facing physical, mental or emotional traumas or disabilities. While members may at one time or another deal with such challenges, the peer exchange groups mentioned in this guide are ongoing and most often will be constituted of members who share some professional or personal interest.

One of the early iterations of peer exchange groups was Napoleon Hill's Mastermind concept. In his book, *Think and Grow Rich*, he describes the power of a weekly meeting with a group of peers and the profound impact this group has on its members' success. In addition to the organization that still operates under Napoleon Hill's name, there are a number of spin-off groups – some of which have been challenged as having misrepresented themselves as part of the Hill organization – using the Mastermind approach. In the business world today, there are also a number of companies that either train leaders for or set up (or both) proprietary peer group organizations, the two best-known probably being TEC (*www.teconline.com*) and Renaissance Executive Forums (*www.executiveforums.com*). I have great respect for all of these organizations, because they too are supporting the peer group concept that I and so many others have found to be so powerful.

During the last 50 or so years, though, other organizations also have been formed to capture this richness for a wide variety of professional groups, some as part of trade associations or professional societies, some under the aegis of religious or value-based organizations, and some as individuals who have been encouraged to become involved in what is most often called a "personal board of directors." These are the organizations and individuals with whom I have worked. The purpose of this book is to outline in a simple way how such groups are formed and operate successfully, so that whether you are new to the process or seeking to revitalize or enrich a group to which you already belong, you can find what you need.

It's not uncommon to hear a member of a vital peer exchange group insist that the learning and personal expansion the group offers has changed his or her life. In fact, among the more than 1,200 groups in 21 countries with which I've worked, such statements are reasonably frequent.

My purpose in creating this guide is simple: to bring that richness to more people in more places and to sustain it where it already exists. And, of course, I owe heartfelt thanks to my own peer support group for their help. I most heartily practice what I preach.

Mo Fathelbab

CHAPTER ONE:

Who Belongs and Why

 eer exchange groups (PEGs) come in various shapes and sizes. Members may have a lot in common because of a shared passion or past. They are just as likely, though, to seem totally diverse, brought together originally by membership in a sponsoring organization and kept together by the value they gain from the experience. Regardless of the composition, one of the first things that affects the group's success is who the members are, how they are selected, and how many there are.

The commonality that gives individuals a reason to come together and commit time, energy and resources to this endeavor can be cause-based, such as any of the myriad groups that use peer exchange to enhance the effectiveness of their local affiliates. It can be role-based, such as a group of CEOs, or it can be generated by membership in a sponsoring organization, such as a Newcomers Club. While the cause-based group may have little commonality of background, education, income level, or profession, initially at least the members have a clearly defined issue to address. Conversely, the role-based group will share a profession and probably also have much more in common in terms of background, education, and income level, but at first won't necessarily all have the same clearly defined reason for joining. Sponsored groups, of course, can vary all along this spectrum. Newcomers, for example, might have geography in common and little else.

While this book will primarily focus on role-based groups, please recognize that many of the tools shared will be of benefit to all kinds of PEGs. The emphasis here is on role-based groups since it is in that arena that I and the other professionals at Forum Resources Network primarily work. Whether because of the financial resources at their disposal or their comfort with using consulting professionals, chief executives and other senior business leaders are our most regular and enthusiastic clients. They know the benefits available from PEGs and eagerly seek to preserve and enhance them. Other groups are often more reticent, at least until they have engaged in the first consulting project. Obviously, one of my purposes here is to overcome that hesitation so that PEGs can work their particular brand of magic on all levels of the socioeconomic spectrum and among all cultures and kinds of people.

Who is a peer and what makes a strong peer group?

Typically, in role-based groups members discuss a wide range of topics, which naturally results in a greater variety of experience to be shared. Without a defining issue to provide focus, the quality of the exchange is particularly dependent on the comfort members have in the peer-to-peer exchange. Simply put, members need to see their peers as peers. Groups like dentists, with members from the same profession, have already narrowed one crucial definition. To create a robust group, it is important that the dentists make sure other dimensions — age, gender, race, geography, and even specialization — are more broadly delineated.

Personality assessments also can be a particularly effective tool in creating a diverse peer exchange group. Using a professionally administered and evaluated measure can help assure that the group is achieving complementary points of view and a richer exchange of ideas.

In the end, since success depends on the comfort of the members, every member needs a voice. When groups are first formed, members have too little information on which to act and also have no knowledge at all of how the group culture will evolve. Over time, an environment will evolve and members will most likely be eager to maintain that environment. That means creating an agreed-upon process for recruitment, a way of dealing with difficulties between members should they arise, and ultimately, a way of dismissing a member who, for whatever reason, may not be a fit. Each of these issues will be addressed in the pages to come.

How big is too big, and how small is too small?

Size matters. Obviously, a small number means greater intimacy, while a larger group expands the knowledge base. Too small and the group will suffer in terms of content and may quickly die from natural attrition. Too large and administrative complexities – who can meet when and where – crop up. There is no magic number, but there is a range that works well.

I've seen groups work effectively with as few as six members and as many as 12. The optimal size is somewhere between eight and 10 members. This does not mean that aiming for the perfect group size should supersede having the right people. One bad apple really does spoil the cart.

Not long ago, a group forming in the US had handily chosen nine members and held a formation retreat — the best possible way to get off on the right foot. (More later.) The retreat was such a great experience for the lucky nine that word spread among the members of the organization sponsoring the PEG; and before those nine could congregate for their first regular meeting, three more candidates contacted the newly-appointed group leader. On paper all three were good possibilities. A delegation of four PEG members — purposely excluding the group leader — took each prospective member to lunch over a period of two weeks. Their task was to select one of the three, since at the retreat the group had decided to limit its membership to 10, at least for the first two years of operation.

To preserve the confidentiality of my client and to make this story easier to tell, let's just say the sponsoring organization was a group of health practitioners, all of them running small practices, either as sole proprietorships or partnerships, none affiliated with a major health care organization. Geographically, they were spread over about 150 square miles. You can see that three lunches in two weeks is a hefty time commitment for busy people, some of whom have to spend more than an hour just getting to the appointment and back. You can also correctly assume that most were below the age of 45, so the profession and the age of the candidates is basically a given. What, then, does the Group of Four look for? Racial/ethnic/diversity, maybe, but in this case the original formation had addressed that issue fairly successfully. Personality? Even the best of us would be just a bit foolish to assume that can be assessed between the appetizer and the coffee. What then?

Back with their report, the quartet was just that. Each person had developed his or her own assessment, but when they spoke it became apparent that already the sense of the group had created four distinct voices singing in harmony.

Amy, the youngest and most outspoken, went first. She found all three prospects acceptable, one definitely more than the other two. "I particularly liked how up-front Joel is," she explained, "and his sense of humor could be a real leavening element for us."

Brent, bespectacled and given to twirling his marbleized pen in his left hand, agreed. "Great guy," he mused, "but if I were forced to choose I think I'd slightly prefer Derek, simply because he's got all that experience with the experimental side of this business. None of the rest of us can begin to know what he does, and we may soon want to."

Kent, the conciliator among not only the four interviewers but the whole PEG, nodded. "Yep, 'tis true. But I gotta tell ya, I've got enough to do just figuring all of you guys out. A comfort zone looks real good to me, and Melanie is just that. She's been with COFHA (the sponsoring organization) longer than most of the rest of us, she knows the ropes and I watched her all during lunch. She really listens."

Finally, Monique spoke. Quiet, determined, but very much a maverick among the group despite her demure exterior, she leaned forward. "Not a single one of those three could really be proven to be bad for us. I liked all three. I think we all did. But we've just emerged from a retreat that, at least for me, says I'm headed into life-bending territory here. I know all eight of you better than I do my brother, and a whole lot better than I ever will my sister. I want time to make the best of what is a fantastic start. It's not my decision, of course, but if it were, I'd say let's get this thing launched and in six months, when we have our next retreat, take a look again. In the meantime, we haven't rejected anybody."

The room was quiet. Invited as my last act as formation consultant, I surveyed the faces. The group leader gave everyone time to think and polled the table for questions. There was some limited discussion, but it was evident that Monique's points held the day. I smiled as I folded the papers into the outside pocket of my laptop case. I hadn't known a person in the room a month before and couldn't have ever predicted this scene at all. How often do nine Type A's say, "Let's wait and see?" They'd definitely been PEGed.

IN BRIEF:

Know what kind of group you want.

Use member input and professional help if you need it to choose your members.

Be small enough to engender good exchange and large enough to expand the wealth of experience.

CHAPTER TWO:
Recruiting Members

ecruiting members for a peer exchange group can be done in several ways. The most natural occurs when a group has an existing affinity. Professional organizations or trade associations, leadership development groups, community-based social action groups, the list is myriad. Members belong to these organizations presumably because they have many of the same challenges and needs. If you already belong to such an organization, you have a natural starting place for forming a PEG.

What if you don't belong to such an organization, but you are eager to participate in a peer exchange group? You are limited only by your own preference. Obviously, for a role-based group, you'll want to look among people who are in your line of work or share your avocation. If you're deeply interested in a cause, chances are you already have found others who share that interest from whom you can recruit. In every case, you can expand your field of possible members by asking others for suggestions.

Here's just a short list of possibilities:

- Explain briefly what you're doing, and ask your lawyer, accountant, doctor, next door neighbor or golf or tennis buddy for suggestions.

- Post a bulletin board notice at your job, community center, health club or local coffee shop.

- Post an ad in the local paper.

- Check out sources of like-minded people on the Internet. Or find a local electronic newsletter for posting a notice.

You'll be amazed at the response you get. I've often worked with individuals forming groups who quickly find they have too many people interested and opt either to turn some down or even to form more than one group.

The process isn't difficult, but it nonetheless requires careful work. It is especially important to watch for conflicts of interest, which we'll discuss in detail in Chapter 8.

It is equally crucial to explain the true nature of a PEG and get buy-in from potential members. More than a decade ago, a group of CEOs who belonged to an organization in a major US city, for purposes of discussion we'll say Chicago, included one person who had moved to the area only six months before from a small, but rapidly growing community where he had been the leading banker. Very successful, principally because of the trust level he had developed with a group of local entrepreneurs, he had been invited to be part of a group leader training session for two very active PEGs operating in the community. What he saw, heard and felt was a departure not only from what he expected, but from anything he had experienced in his professional or even personal life. Now, faced with a new and more diverse professional situation, he very much wanted to see if he could recreate just that situation.

When he presented the idea, there was more than a little skepticism among his Windy City peers, but the executive director of the group saw an opportunity for a new program that might attract new members for the organization and build stronger loyalty among the existing ones. Intrigued, she set up a series of small group familiarization meetings. Some worked, some didn't, but at the end of the eight-week period she used for the project, there were 18 interested (read widely varying levels of enthusiasm here) people. For those 18, she organized two one-day training sessions, and from those sessions emerged two PEGs.

Today, one of them is strong, vital, and meeting regularly, though only two of the original members remain, because the others have moved, changed profession, etc. The other lasted only two years. Why? At the organizing meeting, they decided that the suggested format was not for them. Yes, they would meet monthly. Yes, the agenda would be professionally related. But sometimes, knowing that everyone needs a break from the rough and tumble, they'd just play golf. And other times there were baseball games to attend. In essence, they became a loose amalgam of friends, not a PEG. Friendship is important, but it is not the basis of PEGs. And structure, artificial as it may seem at the outset, is an important underpinning from which springs the true PEG experience.

IN BRIEF:

Suggest peer groups to a professional organization you already belong to and help in the formation.

Solicit potential members from among the people with whom you already share professional or personal interests.

Find recruits by networking or more formal advertising.

Among the different personality assessment tools (and excluding the myriad self-help variety pumped through all kinds of websites), let's look at three of the most potentially helpful.

Probably the most familiar are the Myers Briggs MBTI and its cousin the Kiersey Temperament Sorter, both grounded in the work of Carl Jung. Personalities are described by a set of four opposing pairs: introversion vs. extroversion, thinking vs. feeling, intuition vs. sensing and judging vs. perceiving. Both the informal pop psychology forms of these measures and the more rigorous, predictive and scientifically valid versions are well-known, particularly in the USA. Saying that one is an ENFP is every bit as clear — if loaded — a statement as saying one is a fan of baseball and opera. The strength of the MBTI and related measures is that very familiarity. The weakness, for PEGs, is the emphasis on personal traits/characteristics in some analyses. That's why it is important to assure that a professional administrator/analyst is there to describe how the typology can affect group interaction and communication.

The Enneagram, so named for the nine-pointed diagram that is used as a schematic for its typology, has a devoted following and an equally vociferous set of detractors, principally those who are suspicious of its use in religious or value-based arenas or who disparage its presumed connection with New Age thinking. At the same time, however, it has become a useful tool for leadership development and management consulting. Analyzed and applied correctly for PEGs, it can be somewhat stronger than a strict personality inventory because it measures how group members behave in relation to each other in terms of the nine elements: perfectionism, helpfulness, image awareness, sensitivity, detachment, anxiety, adventurousness, aggressiveness and calmness. Helen Palmer has written extensively on the Enneagram. Another good source for work-related situations is Michael J. Goldberg's book, *The Nine Ways of Working*. There also are several scholars working on how to use the MBTI and the Enneagram in concert.

Finally, the DISC profile is, in my opinion, the strongest measure of any of those I've mentioned here. Introduced in 1928 by William Moulton Marston and developed to be even stronger over time, it is really not a personality inventory as such. It measures behavior in a particular environment in terms of dominance, influence, steadiness and conscientiousness. What can be especially helpful for PEGs is the capacity of the DISC to assess how an individual behaves when he or she is comfortable within a given situation, as opposed to what happens in stressful conditions and what adaptive behaviors are common. The DISC is also especially helpful for making hiring decisions.

There are, of course, multiple others. Better known in academia, the Big Five measures open-mindedness, conscientiousness, agreeableness, emotional stability and extroversion. The TKI, or Thomas Kilman Conflict Mode Instrument, specifies conflict resolution issues. In Europe, both graphology (handwriting analysis) and the Color Quiz developed by Dr. Max Luscher have been included in both hiring decisions and leadership assessment process.

CHAPTER THREE:

Getting Started – First Meeting

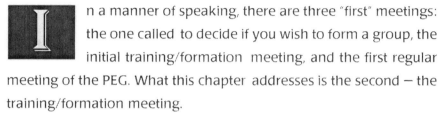

n a manner of speaking, there are three "first" meetings: the one called to decide if you wish to form a group, the initial training/formation meeting, and the first regular meeting of the PEG. What this chapter addresses is the second – the training/formation meeting.

Because of both the length and the intensity of the formation meeting, it is sometimes called a "training retreat." To assure that label is descriptive and not negatively loaded for your prospective members – some people relate retreats to specific religious or meditative traditions with which they are unfamiliar or uncomfortable – it is important to quickly and clearly explain what you're doing.

Whatever the circumstances, your first meeting is critical. By this time, you may be the most comfortable person in the room! For others, this is likely still a new idea, and not everyone will be convinced the PEG idea is a good one. Just as with any relative unknown, some will be skeptical and others will hardly be able to contain their excitement.

Let your members know that during this training session, you will be establishing the ground rules that everyone agrees will make your group work well. Right at the outset, they will learn that the group ethic is one of cooperation and participation peer-to-peer. Yes, if you're wise you'll have a professional trainer there to help, but that trainer's job is to moderate, not to lead. Peers lead peers. There will be no "experts" in your regular meetings.

It's important to have a well thought-out agenda and to let your potential members know in advance how long this initial meeting will last. That, in fact, may be your first hurdle. The typical formation meeting lasts eight to 10 hours, and it is important that everyone can be there the entire meeting. Because that length meeting is definitely not the norm – what other meeting do you know that lasts that long? – your preparation and communication are important.

This initial meeting has four parts. The first addresses the basic issues of formation, the second defines the schedule and logistics of operation for the coming year and the third focuses on planning for the first regularly scheduled meeting. One way to see it is that you are first deciding who you are and how you will proceed, and then you're actually executing what you've decided. Fourth, finally and very important, you will want to include activities that begin group bonding in earnest. These can be activities or exercises embedded in one or more of the other three parts of the meeting, or scheduled completely separately. There are several examples later in this book.

Interestingly, the strongest agenda essentially reverses the order of these four parts by beginning with the bonding exercise and moving to logistics and organizational plans.

Ready...

In addition to the all important business of introducing the members to each other and giving them good, solid ways to get to know each other better, there are important decisions to be made about how the group will operate. Essentially, you will need to draft a confidentiality declaration and delineate member expectations. Let's look at each of those briefly.

Introductions: Just as you would in any new group, you begin with introductions. Unless ALL the members already know each other, the best approach is the simplest -- asking each person to tell his or her name, profession, business, marital relationship, children's ages if any, and hometown. If everyone already is acquainted, you can use a technique that establishes what you have in common. For example, if you all belong to a trade or professional organization, you can state your name and how long you've been affiliated.

Alternatively, and in my experience really successfully, you can ask members of a group who already know each other well, to reveal something that no one else in the room is likely to know at all. Believe me, the results are amazing. Hearing that the most successful female business leader in your industry worked her way through undergraduate school setting pins in a bowling alley changes a meeting.

Confidentiality Declaration: While you'll want to spend a good amount of time getting to know each other better (see below), it's important to assure the comfort of every member before you go any further. Nothing is more fundamental to the operation of a PEG than confidentiality, and it should be the first item on your agenda once everyone has been introduced. In Chapter 7, you'll find all you need to know on how to go about establishing the confidentiality that makes for total member comfort. For now, just know that it comes first!

Member Expectations: Next, I like to give people the opportunity to articulate why they've joined the group and what they expect to get from it. This allows for developing commonality and inclusion. And, it is an early opportunity to flush out any concerns or misunderstandings your potential members may have.

The experience of one group makes this point really well. All of the right work had preceded the first meeting with these people. Most had known each other a while. The organization sponsoring the PEG was a very traditional and well-respected one in the community, and they had contacted a professional trainer early in the game to get her counsel on how to create the group from a position of strength. And they explained the business climate to her, only in the last five or so years had there been any real influx of new business. Two new industrial plants and the very rapid recent growth of the small university in the town had changed the complexion a bit, but not so much that there seemed to be any concern on the part of even the most seasoned among them.

At the initial meeting of the new PEG, though, one of the most senior members, whom we'll call Henry, when asked to say what he expected from the group, leaned back and tucked his thumbs behind his belt. "As you know," his eyes scanned the group, "I'm the fourth generation of my family in this town. When I was a young man, I really thought I'd leave. But then life (in this case polio) changed things, and here I am. It's a change that I now know was good. But I watch what's going on, and I see that in the next 10 years this will be a place my grandfather wouldn't recognize. I'm here because I want to make sure that I'm more like my grandson than my grandfather."

No one in the room, of course, could fault that motive on the face of it. The issue at hand was that his motive and the mission of the PEG did not fit snugly at all. The PEG had been created neither to resist nor to welcome community change, but instead to strengthen the professional and personal lives of every member. It could, of course, be argued that this very respected community member had simply articulated his expectations in a less theoretical and more practical frame. But, with counsel and no small amount of courage, the group leader recognized that this was an issue to clarify early rather than late. He allowed all the others to articulate their expectations and then skillfully led the group in weaving a cohesive whole. When it became apparent to Henry that he was not aligned with the group agenda, he reconsidered.

Getting to Know You: Now we're ready to get to know the other members a little better. The exercises you'll find in Chapter 11 have been used with success by a wide variety of groups. You'll see that some of these exercises are quite deep and others are more informational.

You have the opportunity to choose whichever one you think will work best with your group, but in my experience in training groups all over the world, I've found that for this first meeting the *Ungame* and *My Life Story* work best, in that order. I ask each person to answer a question chosen at random from the *Ungame*. (There is a board version of the game, clearly not appropriate in this setting. I have found that the cards work quite well independently as stimulators of discussion and shared communication.)

While these exercises alone don't make for truly getting to know someone, you'll be amazed at how much some people share and how much you get to know the members of the group. When done correctly and when the group has chemistry, this can be very powerful and result in a relatively quick bonding experience. Not uncommonly, one person who decides to frankly discuss a challenge he or she has faced can completely engage the entire group and create an environment of total trust.

One powerful example comes to mind. The basic details of this story, like the others in this book, have been changed to protect the confidentiality of the group and its members. This particular group was in a culture not all that different from mine, but not one in which I've lived, so not totally familiar either. (It may help you to know that my lineage is Egyptian, and my experience almost totally American.) The group was a little slow getting off the ground, but seemed to be finding its sea legs at long last. Eight of the ten members had flipped over their Ungame card and answered the question, some responses longer than others, but all clearly quite honest. Next to last was a man who exuded leadership from every pore. His ready sense of humor and self-deprecating manner made him a favorite, and his success brought him no small measure of admiration. Now, he stared at the card, bent the corners surprisingly gently and cupped the small oblong in his not at all small hand. He looked up and hesitated. After a deep breath he began.

"I was 10 and it was the end of summer. I'd been at my family's vacation home for more than a month. My uncle had come the weekend before, and I had hardly been able to contain myself until he got there. He was everything I wanted to be: tall, accomplished, genial, never overbearing, funny — a wonderful man who didn't seem to know he was so widely admired. His work as an artist was gaining him notoriety all over Europe, but it never made him pretentious or haughty. On this afternoon, I was sitting on the pier, dredging my not very clean feet in the murky water. He sat down next to me, and in the beginning we talked in the way we had for as long as I could remember (and not nearly so often as I wanted to). Then, in what seemed to be at first just a warm and loving gesture, he put his hand on my thigh. I don't want to and won't talk about the rest. But my answer today to this question is that I have two fears, twined together. One is that I will not be able to continue to keep that secret from the rest of my family. The other is that somehow, because of our shared genes or in reaction to the experience — you can't imagine how much I've read about this — I myself will do something similar. It's not a part of me that I know or would recognize were it to arise. But, I cannot help but fear that somehow, someday, it might."

Just as gently as he had gripped it, he then turned his card over and placed it face down on the table. The effect on his peers cannot be adequately described — or at least I don't feel competent to describe it. This is only one, though, of many such instances of how powerful the Ungame can be.

The Presentation: Often the central part of every meeting, including the training meeting, is a presentation. If any member of the group already has experience with a PEG, it is wise to ask that member to make the presentation. If not, the leader or trainer can work with a designated member on the presentation. While the process will be new, the experience of participating in a presentation teaches more than any amount of explanation or any number of guidelines. Several of the following chapters offer pointers on how to maximize the effectiveness of presentations.

Set. . .

Now it's time to get down to business. You'll need to decide precisely how you're going to operate as a group and then determine what issues you plan to deal with in the coming months.

Ground Rules of Membership: This is not an exercise that sounds like much fun, but it's one that sets the stage for you to go forward smoothly. You'll find a tried and true approach on how to proceed in Chapter 6, complete with samples. In a relatively short discussion, your group can deal with each point and vote on what makes sense for your particular situation.

Member Issues: Having agreed on how you will work together, you now can turn to determining what you will discuss in your upcoming meetings. To go at this in an organized, but not limiting way, and make sure that from the very beginning the whole group is participating, I like to ask each person to share the biggest personal, family and professional challenges he/she is facing.

Once I've listed every member's issues on a flip chart or a white board, the group then works to put them in priority order. This is precisely the method the group leader used to deal with Henry's stated objectives in the case I mentioned earlier in this chapter. An effective way to go about this is explained in detail in Chapter 12. Whether you use that method or one of your own, you should definitely finish this part of the meeting having decided which issue(s) will be covered at your next meeting, and preferably the next two or three.

Go!

Whew! The spadework is now all done, and you're set to take up the logistical decisions. While this is an easy task on the face of it, busy contemporary life can make it more time consuming than you may have believed. Again, there are guidelines in the coming chapters for you, but be sure that before your meeting ends you have appointed a leader — usually called a group leader — and decided when and where you will meet for at least the next six months.

Also, for the next meeting at least, you need to decide which members will be responsible for the following:

Coach — meets prior to the meeting with the member who is making a presentation to (1) help make sure all preparation is completed, and (2) clarify what the presenter wishes to get from the session.

Timekeeper — keeps the meeting on schedule, notifying anyone who is speaking, be it during the updates, the presentation, the questions and answers, or the response period when his/her time is nearly up.

Host — When the group meets in the office of one of its members, this is defined more or less by default. When there is a consistent meeting place, such as a room within a professional club or at an organization's headquarters, one member will be responsible for assuring appropriate room setting, food and beverages, etc.

Finally, as you will learn as the group matures, a structured way of closing can be a big help. It gives members a sense of completion and very often captures the essence of the meeting in a way that other exercises don't. You may have heard a teacher, journalist or counselor argue that frequently the real "meat" of a conversation is found in a closing, oh-by-the-way comment. The same is true of a PEG.

At this first meeting, I like to ask members if their expectations have been met. I also like to ask them to share a sentence reflecting on the day.

Now you have completed your first meeting successfully and you're ready to take your group through an exciting journey.

IN BRIEF:

Help your members get to know each other and define what they want from your PEG.

Decide on how you will work together and what issues are important to you right now.

Choose your leader, set your schedule and head for the future.

Training Meeting Agenda

3:00pm   **Confidentiality Reminder**
Assign roles *(Timer, Scribe, Process Observer)*
Each member to share a thought as a reflection on the
one-day training program

3:10pm   **Updates Prep**

3:20pm   **Updates Share** *(4 min each)*
Parking Lot Build

4:10pm   **Break**

4:15pm   **Develop Group Mission**
What is our purpose?
What will we provide so that our clients and prospects
choose us instead of the competition?

4:45pm   **Develop Group Constitution**

5:15pm   **Elections (Group leader, Secretary, Treasurer)**

5:20pm   **Break**

5:30pm   **Review Presentation Format**
One-Word Open
Confidentiality Reminder
Communication Starter *(30 sec/person)*
Presenter Purpose *(1 min)*
Does Group Understand Purpose/Is It Clear
Presenter Presents *(15 min max)*
Q & A *(30 min max)*
Silence *(3 min)*
Experience Sharing *(3 min/person)*
Presenter Summary *(3 min)*
One-Word Close

5:35pm   **Presentation**

6:45pm   **Housekeeping**
Scheduling meetings for next 6-12 months
Schedule next retreat
Presenter and Coach confirmation for next meeting
What worked and what did not? Go around the room
and ask each person, "what worked, and what
didn't about today's meeting?"

7:00pm   **Adjourn**

CHAPTER FOUR:

Creating Alignment – Mission

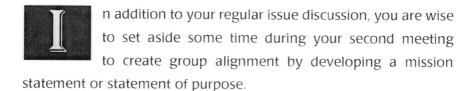 n addition to your regular issue discussion, you are wise to set aside some time during your second meeting to create group alignment by developing a mission statement or statement of purpose.

Why now and not as part of the first meeting? To begin with, that first meeting is already loaded with lots of decision-making, and you don't want to overload it. More important, though, is that all of the members will now have had some time to assimilate what went on in the formation meeting. It could be, for example, that someone wants to discuss or maybe even slightly change the ground rules. It's good to be sure that part of this second meeting will accommodate that, without actually calling for it. And as you talk about what your mission is, these issues can easily be incorporated and conflicts can be flushed out and dealt with in ways that assure the ongoing strength of the group.

Here, too, you move from the individual statement of expectations in the first meeting to a decision as to what the group can and will do. You are in effect giving every member yet another chance to clarify what he/she hopes to achieve through participation in the group.

You are drafting a mission statement that is concerned with the way the group is managed today. It can remain relatively stable, though it should be reaffirmed very regularly (at least annually). A clear and exciting mission statement is a source of strength not only for the group as a whole, but for every member.

Your Mission Statement:

■ Refers to the present or near future (12 months to three years).

■ Describes your group purpose by answering the questions: To do what? For whom? and To what end?

■ Affects decision-making not only on what should be done, but on what should not be done.

■ Promotes a sense of shared purpose.

■ Motivates your group – keep it active in voice and language.

■ Recognizes the different interests of members, and assures they are not in conflict.

■ Identifies the needs of members clearly enough that you can judge the success of the group's performance.

■ Focuses on results and outcomes.

To simplify, I like to think of the mission statement in the following terms:

The mission of <u>name of group</u>;
Is to (<u>what we aspire to do</u>);
Whom (<u>members</u>);
To what end.

An example of a mission statement for a peer exchange group for the divorced might be:

"The mission of the Next Timers is to share, listen and support our members to provide them with opportunities for hope, confidence and personal growth."

In this example, the group's name is the Next Timers. What they aspire to do is to share, listen and support. For whom, is for their members. To what end, is to provide them with opportunities for hope, confidence and personal growth.

In the process of creating the mission statement, you may find that not everyone is aligned. Going back to our Next Timers example, one member may have been hoping to join the group to meet a boyfriend or a girlfriend. While there's nothing wrong with that purpose, and it may even seem to help that one member with hope and personal growth, it may not fit with the other members' intention for the group. It could be that the Next Timers is not the right group for this particular member.

Avoiding this type of misunderstanding is an important result of deciding on a mission statement, and why you need to remember that you're deciding both what you are using the group for and what you are not. This is one place your professional trainer can be particularly helpful.

Sample Mission Statements:

- To build a group of CEOs committed to personal and professional growth.

- To provide a safe environment where we can share openly in order to learn and support one another.

- To share best practices with a group of non-competing professionals dedicated to success.

IN BRIEF:

Set aside time in your second meeting to develop a mission statement.

Take an active approach to defining who you are, what you hope to do, for whom and toward what end.

Make sure all members are aligned with the group's mission as you've defined it.

CHAPTER FIVE:

Meeting Frequency, Length and Timing

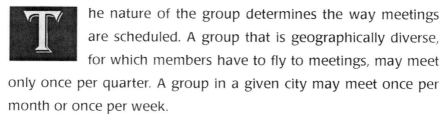he nature of the group determines the way meetings are scheduled. A group that is geographically diverse, for which members have to fly to meetings, may meet only once per quarter. A group in a given city may meet once per month or once per week.

Groups that meet once per month usually schedule their meetings for three to four hours. Start times vary according to the preference of the members. Many of the groups with which I've worked — and I personally — prefer to begin meetings in the late afternoon or early evening and end by about 7 pm. This provides flexibility with an optional dinner after the meeting or alternatively allows people to be home at a reasonable hour to have dinner with their families. It also allows members to have a full day of work prior to the meeting, and therefore clears the way for easier concentration on the group issues at hand.

For groups that meet quarterly, four hours is just not enough time to warrant the trip or to cover all the issues. Here we've found that a two-day meeting works well. This, of course, includes time out for meals and activities. Groups who follow this schedule usually are most effective when they arrive for dinner on day one, work the next two days, and leave before dinner on the second day. Again, this can certainly be modified to meet specific needs, but this schedule is one that has proven effective for a number of groups I've counseled.

For those groups that meet weekly, a two- to three-hour meeting is sufficient. Again, it is up to the group to determine day and time, based on members' schedules and preferences.

No matter what the meeting schedule, it is very important to avoid losing continuity, which can occur if meeting regularity is interrupted. Whether the group meets weekly, monthly or quarterly, canceling a meeting can and most probably will have a negative effect on the members' ability to reconnect.

IN BRIEF:

1. Determine meeting frequency so that you can accomplish your mission and at the same time assure regular attendance by all members.

2. Take into account the frequency when you decide on the length of the meetings – the less frequent the meeting the more time you need.

3. Maintain continuity.

CHAPTER SIX:

Ground Rules of Membership

elieve it or not, I prefer to live my personal life without rules. I'd be surprised if you and the other people who are reading this book wouldn't say the same thing. Still, we all admit that our world needs some rules in order for us to co-exist. So, too, with your PEG. My experience is that having no rules is a dangerous way to run these groups. Better to accept that than to test it by trying to proceed without rules at this stage.

Much as in a partnership agreement, the rules of membership are discussed and agreed to by all members in advance. They include the full range of issues, from cell phone usage to attendance, to what happens when someone breaches confidentiality.

Having the rules discussed and written down before the group actually begins is one way of assuring that personal preferences or idiosyncrasies do not get in the way of group cohesion in unforeseen ways.

The following are a couple of samples of what some groups have done:

Bald Eagles PEG Constitution

This constitution is to be reviewed at the beginning of every meeting.

Mission: To enhance the personal and professional lives of our PEG members through sharing of experience.

Quorum: A quorum is 80 percent of the number of members in the group.

Voting: Decisions are to be made if there is a quorum and if 75 percent of members in attendance agree on the decision. Exceptions can be determined by the group by a vote in accordance with standard voting procedure.

Fiscal Year: April 1 to March 30.

Bald Eagles PEG Norms

1. **Punctuality**
   a. Tardiness or early departure of less than 15 minutes counts as a ¼ absence.
   b. Tardiness or early departure of more than 15 minutes counts as a ½ absence.

2. **Attendance**
   a. A member who misses three meetings within one year will be dismissed from group.
   b. A member who misses a retreat will be dismissed from group.
   c. Call-ins are allowed when scheduling is irreconcilable and when planned in advance.

3. **There will be no use of cellular phones or beepers during meetings – beepers may be set on vibrate mode.**

4. **Retreats will be held annually and will feature a formal agenda.**

5. **All communication will be conducted through email with Bald Eagles in the subject line.**

6. **Roles**
   a. Group leader — one year term. Group leader runs meetings and oversees group progress and serves as back-up secretary.

   b. Secretary — one year term. Secretary handles the business of running the PEG, keeps track of tardiness and absences and serves as back-up group leader.

   c. Communication Protocol Observer — one year term. Checks protocol first three meetings and then every third meeting.

   d. Timer — one year term. Gives warning and notice as instructed by group leader.

7. **Confidentiality**
   "Everything that's said in PEG is confidential; discussion outside PEG must be declared."

8. **Food/Booze**
   a. No drinking before or during monthly meetings.
   b. No eating during presentations or serious portions of meeting.
   c. Drinking at retreats is only during designated times.

9. **Group size: 8-12**

10. **New members must meet unanimous consent of group.**

11. **Members resigning are to make an exit presentation.**

12. **Group will follow the language protocol as follows:**
    a. During presenter's opening segment, use "I" statements.
    b. During Q&A, explain your question before asking it.
    c. During summary, speak from experience — past tense.

13. PEG Experience
"Each member of PEG is responsible for his/her own PEG experience."
a. Be the first to share.
b. Be proactive when you have a problem.

14. Meeting format/frequency
a. Frequency —12 meetings per year including retreat
b. <u>Format</u>
    3:00pm- Review and agree upon agenda
    3:15pm- Best & Worst (business & personal) 4 min. each
    Break
    4:15pm- Presentation
    5:45pm- Housekeeping: Membership, attendance, etc.
    What worked and what did not?
    6:00pm- Adjourn

15. Presentation Format
Presenters to be determined one month in advance — group leader to determine exceptions.
a. Remind group of confidentiality.
b. 30-second warm-up.
c. Presenter indicates in one minute, what he/she expects from the group.
d. Group leader repeats the presenter's objective ensuring group understanding.
e. Presenter describes the situation without interruption in 20 minutes or less.
f. Question and answer period, group leader calls upon members in the order in which they raise their hands (no more than 40 minutes).
g. Summary — this is where each member of the group gives his/her relevant experience, that which answers the presenter's objective in two to three minutes. The first person to speak is the person to the immediate left of the presenter. The last person to speak is the presenter.

It is critical that this step is in a strict clockwise order with no interruptions and that there is not interaction or rebuttal after each summary — the presenter will get the last word.

h.   One-word close.
i.   Presentation is over.

16. Emergency Meetings

Attendance if possible. In case of scheduled meeting, group leader makes decision.

Blackwood PEG Constitution

This constitution is to be reviewed at the beginning of every meeting.

Mission: Gain perspective and intellectual and emotional stimulation from committed peers who share experiences in a safe and structured environment.

Fiscal Year: Fiscal year is July 1 to June 30.

Blackwood PEG Norms

1.   **Punctuality -- $100 penalty for tardiness up to 30 minutes, after 30 minutes it is counted as an absence.**

2.   **Attendance**
a.   A member who misses two meetings within a fiscal year will be dismissed from group.
b.   A member who misses a retreat will be dismissed from group.
c.   A member may be reinstated by unanimous consent.

3.   **There will be no use of cellular phones or beepers during meetings – may be set on vibrate mode.**

4.   **Members must bring calendars to all meetings.**

5.   **PEG will attempt to have one retreat per year.**

6.   **Group leader – one-year term. Group leader runs meetings, oversees group progress and serves as back-up secretary. Group leader must attend group leader training.**

7.   **Confidentiality**
"Everything that's said in PEG is confidential, discussion outside PEG must be declared as confidential." A member who has breached confidentiality is automatically dismissed from group unless unanimously reinstated.

8.   **Group size: 8 minimum**

9.   **New members must meet unanimous consent of group.**

10. **Members resigning are to make an exit presentation.**

11. **Group will follow the language protocol as described below.**

13. PEG Experience
"Each member of PEG is responsible for his/her own PEG experience."

14. Attempt to hold meeting monthly.

15. Presentation Format
Presenters to be determined one month in advance – group leader to determine exceptions.
a. Remind group of confidentiality.
b. 30 second warm-up.
c. Presenter indicates in one minute what he/she expects from the group.
d. Group leader repeats the presenter's objective ensuring group understanding.
e. Presenter describes the situation without interruption in 20 minutes or less.
f. Question and answer period: group leader calls upon members in the order in which they raise their hands (no more than 40 minutes).
g. Three minutes of silence.
h. Summary: this is where each member of the group gives his/her relevant experience, that which answers the presenter's objective in 2 to 3 minutes. The first person to speak is the person to the immediate left of the presenter. The last person to speak is the presenter. **It is critical that this step is in a strict clockwise order with no interruptions and that there is not interaction or rebuttal after each summary – the presenter will get the last word.**
i. One-word close.
j. Presentation is over.

16. Emergency Meetings – Attendance if possible. In case of
scheduled meeting, group leader makes decision.

Bradley Springfield Group Constitution

Mission:
Network, support and energize members for the purpose of motivation, learning, profitability and success.

Confidentiality:
- Be able to share with staff
- Don't share with another contractor in the area
- All numbers/books are confidential
- Share with spouse and owners

Attendance:
If a member misses two meetings in a row, he/she is out of the group. Members who are thereby dismissed are still responsible for their share of costs, including facilitator fees.

Food/Booze: There will be no drinking of alcohol during sessions.

Group size: 8-12

Membership: Owners, non-union, non-competing, non-consolidator, independent contractor, household service must be part of business and company must be a member of at least one of the three professional associations. New members must meet unanimous consent of the group prior to meeting and the group has a right of refusal after meeting.

Members resigning: Must send a letter to all group members 90 days prior to next meeting, and are responsible for fees for the next meeting.

Language Protocol: Members are to speak from experience.

PEG Experience: Each member is responsible for his/her own experience.

Meeting Schedule: Meetings are held twice per annum.

Logistic Support: ABC to handle group facilitation and meeting planning. This to be evaluated at the end of each meeting.

Member Participation/Communication: Members are encouraged to contact each other between meetings. Members must bring their schedule to each meeting.

IN BRIEF:

The key to a successful set of rules is the democratic process the group uses to arrive at the rules.

Each member must buy in and agree in advance.

CHAPTER SEVEN:
Confidentiality

B y their very definition, peer exchange groups are self-defined. That means nearly every element can vary — qualification for membership, mission, schedule of meetings, etc. The one element that is central for a strong group, no matter how mission, structure and norms vary, is agreed-upon confidentiality. It is the underpinning of the kind of safe environment that enables members of a group to share openly and honestly.

While a confidentiality clause doesn't guarantee that there won't be violations, it certainly provides an understanding and a level of expectation of each member. And, as is obvious in the different ways confidentiality is defined in the sample constitutions in the preceding chapter, the level of confidentiality can vary.

The challenge is that some things that are shared simply seem benign and harmless, while other things are far from it. When a member announces that he/she is moving across the country, it may seem as if there should be no reason the information could not be public knowledge. On the other hand, it may be that this person has not revealed these plans to co-workers, family or friends.

The most common — and by far the best — rule for confidentiality is: "Nothing, no one, never."

So you ask, what about that person moving across the country? What if I know a mutual friend who brings it up, do I pretend not to know anything? How do I handle these situations?

Nothing means that members of the group cannot share anything regardless of how trite or seemingly benign.

No one means that members of the group cannot share information provided in the group setting with anyone. This includes spouses, best friends and/or professional counselors.

Never means that even after a member is no longer a member or even if this is something that occurred 10 years ago, it is still confidential.

If you hear something and you think it may in fact be not confidential, you may simply ask the person who shared it. "Is this confidential?" The answer may be "no," or "my best friend knows but my parents don't." Then, based upon that, you can act accordingly.

What about dealing with issues outside group meetings? For example, Mary tells her group that she's considering a divorce. Can Mary talk about this issue with her parents? The answer is obviously yes. However, Mary cannot share with her parents what members of the support group shared about themselves.

The examples of how important the confidentiality agreement is are rife, but for purposes of brevity, let me describe only one in full detail, and then a few others briefly to emphasize just how important TOTAL confidentiality can be. Also, please remember that because I, too, am bound by confidentiality and know — keenly know — how crucial it is, these examples, like all of the others in this book, have been changed enough so that they are not traceable to actual situations.

The first example involves a PEG that we will call the Ladder Eleven that had been in existence for some time, long enough that the members had become particularly close. It operated under the aegis of a professional organization that was large enough that it sponsored 37 PEGs in its 10 chapters. Four were affiliated with the chapter Ladder Eleven operated within, one other for members and two for the spouses and significant others of members.

Each October, the organization made arrangements so that all four groups could hold their meetings on the same day in close geographical proximity, and then join the overall organization for its annual Founders' Day dinner party. This particular year, Ed, a member of the Ladder Eleven, had asked for extra time during the update segment of the meeting. Wanting to make sure Ed had all the time he needed, the group leader scheduled his update last. As the other members went through their own updates, he became more and more anxious, agitated and strangely quiet, since he was the most jovial member of the group. Finally, when his term came, he clamped one fist inside the other, leaned forward, and said in a raspy voice, "Last Thursday, Scott tried to commit suicide."

While the statement was terse and unsettling, the lack of explanation was not as stark as it might have been. The Ladder Eleven group knew all about Scott, the very talented and troubled 18-year-old son of their peer. This was not the first problem they'd heard of, but it certainly was the most severe. As the anguished father went on to detail the discovery of his son's situation and the wrenching trip to the psychiatric hospital 25 miles away that followed, they together offered every ounce of attention and support they could muster. While the meeting eventually turned to the formal presentation, everyone clearly remained concerned and vigilant, while Ed relaxed somewhat but participated far less actively than normal.

The meeting over, the group moved on to the Founders' Day dinner. There Amelia, the newest of the Ladder Eleven and a particularly sensitive woman, spotted Dorothy, Ed's wife, who came in with the members of her own PEG. Waiting for the appropriate opportunity — that is, when no one else was in earshot — Amelia finally stepped next to Dorothy, put her hand on the taller woman's shoulder and said quietly, "Dot, I want you to know how much we all are feeling for what you're going through."

When the color drained from Dorothy's face and she turned and fled, Amelia realized with a sinking feeling her mistake. Unlike her husband, Dorothy had not been able to confide in her PEG cohorts. Not only that, she thought she had an agreement from Ed that he, too, would remain quiet. In her zeal to offer friendship, kindness and support, Amelia had forgotten how firm the confidentiality agreement must be with no exceptions.

Because of her mistake, Ed wrestled with not only a troubled son, but a damaged marital relationship.

What's even more difficult is how to deal with those who, like Amelia, violate the confidentiality agreement. The standard policy that I recommend is that the person who violates confidentiality apologize to the member affected by this breach and offer his/her resignation to the group. The group has the ability to choose not to accept the resignation, but because of the seriousness of the issue, I strongly recommend that this be done only by unanimous consent and either by secret ballot or in the absence of the member who breached.

Obviously, there are likely to be instances when a member who breaches does not follow the above, is not able to admit to the breach or does not want to leave the group. If that is the case and the breach is discovered by another member, it is up to that member to handle the issue using the conflict resolution model in Chapter 14.

A word of caution: The confidentiality clause does not protect members of the group from illegal activity or from seeking professional assistance if a life is in danger. For example, if a member has insider information, members of the group cannot trade company stock based upon that information. The PEG is not above the law. Likewise if a member mentions any intention to take someone's life or his/her own, a professional should be called immediately.

Now, let's look briefly at some other examples of what can go seriously wrong even when intentions are totally positive, and how groups have decided to deal with the issue and/or the offender.

Case #1: But No One Said a Word!

When Joe walked into his office one Tuesday morning, he found his partner irate. "So you're planning to force me out?," his soon-to-be-former colleague accused. The accusation was accurate, but Joe had told no one but his PEG. Livid, he called an emergency meeting to find out who breached confidentiality. Everyone was at the meeting and to a person they claimed innocence and reiterated their concern for Joe. Each of them also insisted that he/she did not reveal Joe's plans to anyone. Joe was in complete disbelief, and he struggled to find any faith in his peers. Everyone was completely soured by the experience yet no one knew what to do. A week later

Joe's partner said, "My wife overheard everything when she was at lunch at Clyde's last week." At which point, Joe remembered that some of his PEG members had gone to lunch at Clyde's around the same time.

What went wrong: The PEG members continued discussing Joe's issue in public. They had good intentions and they were brainstorming ideas for him. They violated the "walls have ears" rule and they were overheard.

What is the resolution: Joe realized that five of the members were discussing his issue at lunch with the best of intentions. Everyone apologized profusely. They learned a big lesson; they stayed together as a group and they reviewed the rules of confidentiality and came to a new understanding and clarity.

Case #2: That Wasn't in PEG!

Judy and Patrick are in a PEG together. At a cocktail party when Judy ran into Patrick and his friend, Tony, she asked Patrick if his girlfriend, Susie, liked the engagement ring. Patrick quickly turned away, but not before she saw the anger in his face. Needless to say the situation became more uncomfortable. The PEG meeting was the very next morning, and Patrick made it clear that he felt Judy had breached confidentiality.

What went wrong: Patrick had called Judy to seek her opinion on diamond rings. He thought that because she was a member of his PEG, their discussions would be confidential. Judy thought nothing of it, because the discussion took place totally outside a PEG meeting. Patrick and Judy had different understandings of whether discussions between two members which originate outside PEG are confidential or not.

What is the resolution: Patrick and Judy discussed the issue with the other PEG members. The group agreed they had no clear rules on discussions that originate outside PEG between two members. They decided that such discussions must be declared as confidential at the time. NOTE: This is strictly for matters brought up outside of the meeting and not about the PEG or its other members. PEG matters are always confidential unless declared otherwise.

Case #3: Technology Bytes

For some time Ken had been dealing with a difficult issue; and it was often his pattern to send emails to the members of the PEG to ask various questions. At one of the meetings, he thanked the members for all their support and responsiveness to his situation, adding a special thanks to Jim, who had been particularly helpful. Jim looked very agitated. The group leader was alert to his discomfort, and when she asked Jim what was wrong, he explained: "I've not responded to any of the emails. That email address is my home account and my whole family shares it."

What went wrong: The PEG had not had a clear discussion on what is to be included in emails to preserve confidentiality. Nor did they discuss privacy of their emails.

What is the resolution: Each member confirmed that he/she has an email address that is private for PEG purposes. Members checked with their IT departments to confirm that their emails are protected when they are backed up on the server. They also confirmed that each of their emails is password protected. Finally they decided that when posting meeting agendas, they no longer publish who is presenting or the topic of presentation.

Case #4: If They Don't Know Who or What

Joanne went home after a PEG meeting very disturbed by Jack's presentation. She proceeded to tell her husband about everything, but made sure she didn't tell him that it was Jack who presented. That same night Barbara's husband asked her what happened in PEG. A very cautious woman, Barbara said I can't tell you that, but I'll just say that Jack presented a serious issue. The next week, when both couples attended the local high school basketball game together, the two husbands started talking and within a few minutes, they knew exactly what was presented and by whom. The cat was out of the bag.

What went wrong: Joanne gave away the story thinking it would never matter because her husband would never know who presented it. Barbara thought she was being very sly in only sharing who presented.

What is the resolution: "Everything that's said in the room stays in the room," means EVERYTHING. Nothing, no one, never! The PEG eventually found out and both Joanne and Barbara were asked to leave.

Case #5: Tip of the Week

Ross was in the printing business. His company specialized in printing annual reports and he would often see an annual report a couple of weeks before it was released to the public. Ross saw the members of his PEG as brothers and sisters and wasn't at all averse to giving them information before it was available to the public. On one occasion, he came across a company that was going to beat estimates by 50 percent — a fact that he excitedly passed on to the other PEG members. Sharing his glee, they all bought the stock. Sure enough, when the annual report came out, the stock soared. Not long after that, Ross received a call from the SEC. Notwithstanding the wonderful humor of the 1998 movie, "Waking Ned Devine," PEGs operate not only under their own regulations, but also very much inside the legal framework of the country in which they live and work.

What went wrong: Insider trading is illegal. While this PEG operated under strict confidentiality, the members broke the law.

What is the resolution: The case is still pending.

IN BRIEF:

Agreed-upon confidentiality is a necessity.

In most cases, the best policy is "nothing... no one... never."

Make sure you have clearly defined the ways of dealing with violations and follow through.

CHAPTER EIGHT:

Conflict of Interest

 onfidentiality is all about creating a safe environment, but in many professional settings, there is a potential problem of conflict of interest. Here, conflict of interest is defined not nearly as exactly as it is in the workplace. What we mean by conflict of interest is anything that will preclude or inhibit a member from sharing openly and honestly with members of the PEG.

In selecting group members, it is important to be attentive to potential conflict of interest "hot spots." In general, it is a good idea to try to avoid:

- Business competitors

- Business partners

- Those conducting business together over time. (Let the group decide if one discrete project should be an issue.)

- Coworkers, be they colleagues or superiors/subordinates

- Personal dating relationships (unless the PEG is a couples group)

- Individuals investing in a PEG member's business

- A lifelong friend of a partner – business or personal

- A lifelong friend of a competitor

The goal in avoiding a conflict of interest is to have a pure environment, in which members have no reason to withhold information due to anything other than their own insecurity, readiness or comfort level to deal with a given issue.

The issue of relationships or situations that may be short-term can be a difficult one, but many PEGs have found constructive ways to deal with them. One situation I experienced is a good case in point. A PEG member I'll call Preston was the executive director of a trade association. While another of the PEG members, whom I'll call Whitt, was also a member of the same trade association, there were no problems until Whitt was elected to the association board. When Preston faced a professional issue on which he wished to make a presentation, he requested that Whitt not attend that meeting. Whitt understood, as did the entire group. Another, similar situation, involved a group in which one member bought a business that is a direct competitor of the business of one of her PEG colleagues. She opted to resign from the PEG. Eager to continue the benefits, she formed a separate group where there would be no conflict of interest.

On the other side of the coin, in countries where there are laws limiting unfair business practices or monopoly, it is important to assure that PEG exchanges in no way abrogate those laws for any member. Insider trading is an obvious case in point, but price fixing and other issues can just as easily arise. Members worried about such issues cannot talk openly.

IN BRIEF:

Create a group where conflict of interest will not be a problem.

If issues arise despite your care in choosing members, let the group determine how to deal with them before they become a problem.

Stay within the law – in letter and in spirit.

CHAPTER NINE:
Language Protocol

nother critical factor in building that all so important safe environment is having the appropriate language protocol.

The language protocol that I have found to be the most effective can be difficult for many. In fact, for some it will be a complete departure from how we've been trained to communicate, but it may well be that it is for those very same people that the language protocol was created.

It is certainly the case that it's not just what we say that matters. How we say it and whether we say it are equally vital if we are to achieve a safe environment where members of the group can share openly and honestly.

No matter what you think, or even what you hear from a friend now and again, the basic truth is that in settings like a PEG, no one actually wants advice. People often ask for advice, but really what they mean is, "I want your help, your support, or your ear." The question is: How can you help without giving your advice or telling someone what to do, or what you think, or what you would do?

It is very tempting to just blurt out, "Here's what you need to do," or "What I think is best," or "There's a solution to this, now…" In the process of doing that, you subconsciously leave the other person with the feeling that you know what's best and/or a concern about how can he/she be so stupid as not to see the answer. Despite your best intentions, you have taken a person who is already vulnerable and diminished another notch or two his/her self-image. Not a result that you are after in PEG – or probably most any other time.

So, you ask, how exactly do we help one another and what is our purpose if we can't give advice? What if the person asks for advice?

Great questions. I can promise you, though, that I've worked with PEGs since 1991, more than 80 percent of them composed of successful corporate CEOs who believe − often accurately − that they know how to deal with all kinds of problems. In every case, I have found there to be no reason to feel you can safely give advice. Let me explain why.

Take a look at how you can help if you can't give advice. During a PEG meeting, a person who brings an issue to the group benefits in many ways.

First, he/she thinks about the issue and prepares the presentation in advance. If there's no reason to worry about being second guessed or otherwise affronted, it's easy to engage in this process straightforwardly. And, no surprise, that itself can provide a good portion of the needed "answer." A little like coming up with an answer the minute you take it out of your head and into the dinner conversation.

Next, the presenter benefits by expressing his/her issue to a group of people who listen, care and are not judgmental. Think about it: where else in your life can you expect that result, no judgmental questions asked? (The presenter benefits most, of course, from thought provoking questions, not those asked to clarify.) And definitely not to be overlooked, if you're worried about the issue and designing your presentation, you're going to think about the questions that members of the group might ask. This provides more upfront clarification, even if those questions are never actually presented.

Finally, the presenter benefits by hearing the experiences of other members of the group. But, don't forget that every PEG member benefits in much the same way. If you give advice, it is specific to the problem being presented. If you talk about your experience, it is a little — or maybe a lot — different. Every listener can then apply it to his or her issues. In some circles, this is called synchronicity. In PEGs, it's called standard operating procedure. And, looking at things from a negative perspective, you also risk alienating yourself from your PEG members if you resist sharing your experiences when the opportunity arises.

Throughout the process no one gives advice. It's simply not necessary and the risks of the damage it can cause are far too great. You risk belittling a person who's already vulnerable, even if he or she is talking about success instead of failure. Either way, the underbelly is up.

- You risk seeming to be a "know it all," and thereby compromise your relationship with other group members and their comfort.

- You lose the possible serendipitous application to the issues other PEG members are thinking about.

- And, most important, you undermine the safe environment that ensures honest, open and complete sharing in the future.

So this is not how you're used to talking? Bet not. Neither am I. But with some practice it's not all that hard to learn. Awkward as it may be in the beginning, your goal is to speak strictly from experience, so you focus on using statements that incorporate the word "I," not "one" or "you." It isn't too often you hear, "One really likes dark chocolate." Nor, unless there is the underlying "Where'd ya get that extra 15 pounds?" message, will you say, "You really like dark chocolate, don't you?" But, "I really like dark chocolate" says you know the feeling. You are telling stories on yourself.

There is yet another refinement. To keep you comfortably within the protocol, your stories are best in the past tense. (Even if you still like dark chocolate.) If you analyze that for a minute, you'll see how it takes your story from being in any way chiding to being a simple explanation of "This is what happened to me. I know it's not exactly the same, but I surely do understand at least some of what you're feeling. And, for what it's worth, this is what I did and it did (or, sometimes better yet, did not) work."

Here's what you **DON'T** say:
"You should really quit smoking."
"If I were you, I'd quit smoking."
"You ought to quit smoking."
"I recommend that you quit smoking."
"I would quit smoking."
"I believe that one should not smoke."

Here's what you **DO** say:

"I used to smoke four packs of cigarettes every day. My doctor said I was going to die if I didn't quit. My husband stopped sitting next to me when I smoked. We had fights every night about my habit. I tried to quit several times, but I always went back to it. Then I saw one of those guys with a hole in his throat and I decided that wasn't for me. I started to use the patch and I was able to quit."

OR

"I still smoke three packs a day, and I often try to quit, but I always go back to it. I've really become addicted to smoking. I know it's not good for me, but I just can't stop. I know what you're going through."

OR

"I have no experience with smoking, but I had an addiction to alcohol. I used to drink every day. Finally, I realized that it was getting out of hand. It was affecting my relationship with my family and my performance at work, and I decided to go to AA. I'd tried to quit drinking before many times, but it turned out I needed a support group of people who understood and who were going through the same thing."

OR

"I have no experience to share with you, but I want to offer my support and my ear anytime. I wish you good luck on your journey."

OR

"I smoked for 10 years and I thought nothing of it. In fact, I thought it was cool. I finally realized that it didn't mix well with my professional image. I also realized that it was just a nervous habit. I used Nicoderm and it really worked. But first I had to make the decision and the commitment."

Yes, following the language protocol takes a little more time, a little more thinking and a lot of practice. But it's worth it. In these examples you heard the message "I share your pain," "I'm not perfect either," and "I'm not passing judgment on you." Whatever the experience, the messages were of comfort, support and caring. Every speaker listened with heart and head.

In much the same way, you can do a lot to improve the question and answer period by watching how you ask questions.

Here's what the smoker has no doubt heard all too often:
"Why don't you just quit?"
"Don't you think you should quit?"
"Don't you know that smoking is bad for you?"

And here is an approach that may actually make a difference:
"How long have you been trying to quit?"
"What products or systems have you tried in your pursuit?"

Finally, no matter how adept you are at choosing your words and following the language protocol, if you are not expressing the way you really feel, there are other parts of the communication process that will give you away. Your tone or your body language can negate your words in short order. What you are about here is actually changing the message you want to send, not the manner of sending it!

One particularly memorable meeting made me realize with startling and life-changing clarity how ineffective even the best advice can be and how powerful a sincerely shared experience is. And this time, it was not an effect I only witnessed, but one I found myself deeply involved in. First, a little background on me.

My parents were divorced when I was three years old, and until I was 11, they fought fierce and bitter custody battles. During those eight years, I saw my dad only three times. Because my mother was concerned that he might kidnap me, I was never alone with my dad. A chaperone always kept a watchful eye. Then I moved to the United States with my mother. When my dad visited, he encouraged me to visit him when I went back to Egypt, and slowly over the next seven years, we began to build a relationship.

Not unlike many other fathers, he started to criticize me for a host of things when I entered my teenage years. It became uncomfortable enough for me that when I turned 18, I decided I no longer needed him in my life. The distances, both emotional and geographic, that had defined our past together made the decision an easy one to make and carry out.

In the decade to follow, members of my mother's family gave me lots of advice aimed at getting me to call my dad. The advice was well intentioned and it came from people I respect and who clearly had my best interests in mind. It did not, however, change my mind.

When I was 25, I became a member of a PEG. Three years later one of our members, whom I'll call Brett, brought to a meeting the eulogy he had delivered at his father's funeral. After reading it to us, he paused, looked up, and added how much he wished he had played with his dad the way other kids he knew had. He added honestly and with no pride how very much he wished his father had acknowledged his (Brett's) success. He concluded by saying how deeply he wished the closeness they had begun when his father lay dying could have begun many years before.

The emotion-laden quiet that followed lasted only a minute or so. Then, one by one, everyone began to talk about their relationships – or lack thereof – with their fathers. The meeting became even more emotional, of course. To a person, everyone was moved. In my case, for the first time I understood – no felt – how much I was missing by staying away from my father. I called him the very next day.

I wasn't the only one who learned, and in fact the learning had almost as much to do with us as a group as it did with each of us as individuals.

We learned that every presentation is an opportunity for us to become closer by learning more about one another – if we share our experience rather than give advice.

We learned that if we want to preserve our egos and keep our distance, we give advice.

We learned that if we want to get close to someone, we share our truth (good, bad and ugly) rather than pass judgment by offering advice and opinion.

We learned that no one wants advice, we just want solutions, but that the person with a challenge is the person with the solution to that challenge. Our job is to ask appropriate questions, and offer our experience.

Most of all, we learned that our PEG is a gift!

IN BRIEF:

Make your message one of support, not judgment. Communicate with "I" messages.

Make your experience useful to every listener — including yourself.

CHAPTER TEN:

Meeting Agendas

Meetings have three main components and last anywhere from three to four hours for a monthly meeting and one to two days for a quarterly meeting. The three major components of a meeting are updates, presentations and housekeeping. In addition, some groups also use warm-up and closure techniques to enhance group dynamics.

Updates

One of the important parts of every meeting is the updates. Updates give members of the group an opportunity to catch up in an organized and meaningful way. Updates are done at the beginning of each meeting and are timed by the timekeeper (a member of the group identified by the group leader) so they do not constitute a rambling session — four to five minutes per person is a good rule of thumb. During updates, it is important to just listen to the member giving the update. Updates are not about random discussions; they are about listening.

There are several ways to conduct updates, and here are some questions you can use to structure your update:

What are the five most significant things that have happened in your life since we last met? These things can be business, personal, and/or family related. It's a good idea to have at least one item from each category.

Forum Resources Network Update Form

	Best	Worst	Dread	Look Forward
Business or Finance or Purpose or Faith				
Family or Relationship w/spouse, kids, siblings, or parents or Love life				
Personal or Mental Health or Physical Health				

What was the high point of your last month? What was the low point? Is there a particular issue with which you struggled? What is it?

Since the last meeting when were you most happy?

Most sad?

Updates can provide a powerful conduit for members of a group when done properly and honestly.

Presentations

After updates are complete, most groups move directly to presentations. A presentation involves a member bringing a specific issue to the group for discussion.

The presentation process has the following main components:

Communication Starters: questions the group responds to in order to get into the presenter's shoes, let him/her know that others have shared similar experiences, reactions and feelings.

Stating the Objective: clear and concise with a focus on only one issue.

Presenting the issue: a detailed explanation of the issue by the member.

Q&A: After the presentation and before the discussion begins, members are given the opportunity to ask questions to help them better understand.

It is important to remember that the questions are focused totally on clarification, and have no element of challenge within them. Basically, these are who and what questions, not why questions.

Sharing experiences: Each member shares an experience that speaks to the objective of the presenter.

Housekeeping

After the presentation(s), the housekeeping segment of the meeting provides the group the opportunity to discuss organizational issues: membership, attendance, punctuality, scheduling, and future presenters.

These meetings can obviously be held any time of the day as long as the time is suitable for everyone.

Forum Resources Network Communication Starters™

Tell us about something mischievous you did as a child.

What were the two most emotional times of your life?

If you could scratch any one day from your life so that it never existed, what day would it be and why?

If you could relive any one day from your life, which day would it be?

Tell us something about yourself that your spouse does not know?

Tell us about the proudest moment of your life? What made it special?

Have you ever hated anyone? Why and for how long?
Tell us about the last time you were in a fight. Who caused it? Who won?

Whose death do you fear most? Why?

Whose death has impacted you the most. How?

If you could communicate with anyone who is dead, who would it be and what would you say?

What is your most treasured memory?

Who do you wish you could talk to in your dreams?

One-Word Open/Close

Some groups, though not all, find it helpful to set the tone at the beginning of the meeting and to check the pulse of the group at the end by polling the group for a one-word description of how each feels. When the meeting agenda is expected to be or has been particularly intense, the one-word poll can be a valuable way of assessing group cohesion and assuring that every member feels included.

First-Meeting Agenda

3:00pm **Confidentiality Reminder**
Assign roles (Timekeeper, Process Observer)
Each member to share a thought as a reflection on
the one-day training program

3:10pm **Updates Prep**

3:20pm **Updates Share** *(4 min. each)*
Parking Lot Build

4:10pm **Break**

4:15pm **Develop Group Mission**
  • What is our purpose?
  • What will we provide so that our clients and
    prospects choose us instead of the competition?

4:45pm **Develop Group Constitution**

5:15pm **Elections** (Group Leader, Liaison to Administrator)

5:20pm **Break**

5:30pm **Review Presentation Format**
  • One-word open
  • Confidentiality reminder
  • Communication starter *(30 sec. per person)*
  • Presenter's purpose *(1 min.)*
  • Does group understand purpose/is it clear?
  • Presenter presents *(20 min. max)*
  • Q&A *(40 min. max)*
  • Silence *(3 min.)*
  • Experience sharing *(3 min. per person)*
  • Presenter summary *(3 min.)*
  • One-word close

5:35pm **Presentation**

6:45pm	**Housekeeping**

- Scheduling meetings for next 6-12 months
- Schedule next retreat
- Presenter and coach confirmation for next meeting
- What worked and what did not – Go around the room and ask each person, "What worked, and what didn't about today's meeting?"

7:00pm   **Adjourn**

CHAPTER ELEVEN:
Exercises and Tools to Build Relationships and Trust

here are many tools that are available to you that can help in building relationships and trust within the PEG. We, at Forum Resources Network, have developed a set of questions that have proven to be particularly successful, and because of that these questions have become our most frequently used tool. Copies are available at no charge for our clients, and may be purchased separately by contacting Forum Resources Network.

Other tools we sometimes recommend include a game and a book. *The Ungame* is a deck of cards with insightful questions that elicit sharing. Developed by a woman who spent a period of time both unable to speak and fearful that she might never speak again, *The Ungame* can be played as a board game, but is used most effectively by PEGs to elicit candid discussion on subjects that, were the questions asked directly, might be considered off limits. Because each person essentially asks him/herself the questions, the feeling of intrusion is avoided.

The book called *If* by James Saywell and Evelyn McFarland has been sufficiently popular that the authors have now written two sequels.

These tools offer quick communication starters to break the ice. In a retreat setting, they also can be used for an extended discussion.

In this chapter you will find some other tools that can be helpful, and have already been used in healthy PEGs – in other words, they're road tested. To make your reading easier and faster, I've written each exercise as directions for you, but in actuality they apply to all PEG members.

My Life Story

Take an hour to prepare this exercise. You may choose to do this in advance or during a meeting. After preparation, take 30 minutes to share your story in chronological order.

To prepare this exercise, here are some things to think of:

- Birthplace and date
- Birth order and relationships with your siblings
- Parents' situation, occupation & relationship
- Schools attended
- Significant accomplishments
- Significant setbacks
- Key relationships
- Jobs held
- Places lived
- Dramatic events
- Big secrets you've never shared
- Whatever else comes to mind

Your Life

What about your life do you like/dislike?

- Work
- Family
- Personal
- Relationships
- Fitness/Health

Tell us about a time when everything seemed to be great.

Tell us about a time when nothing seemed to be working.

How would you like to change the things you don't like?

What can you do to preserve the things you do like?

I Pretend

Tell your group about three things you pretend and why you feel the need to do so. These can be things like:

I pretend to be successful.
I pretend to be rich.
I pretend to be carefree.

The Group would be Surprised to Know....

Here's your opportunity for a revelation to the group. The group leader will begin, and then you and your fellow members will in turn share one thing that the group would be surprised to know about you. Because you're sharing only one thing and many of us have many more to share, this exercise is easily repeated.

My Life's Relationships

Tell the group about the significant romantic relationships in your life. Things to think about:

- Who?
- When?
- What was special?
- What was difficult?
- Why did they end?
- Do you see any patterns in the relationships?
- Do you see any patterns in the types of people you choose?
- Do you have any regrets?
- What have you learned?

This requires 20-30 minutes of preparation and 20 minutes to share.

Life Direction Exercise

Mission – Purpose in Life; what am I on this earth to do?

Each person takes 30 minutes to write
Share Mission with group

Core Values – Personal Principles

Each person to take 10 minutes to list his/her values.
Take another 5 minutes to look at the attached list.
Now think about the following. If I had to narrow the list
down to the most important value, what would it be?
What is the second most important? The third? The fourth?
The fifth? What does each of these values mean to you?
Each person to share his/her values.

SWOT Analysis – What are my strengths, weaknesses,
opportunities & threats?

This is another way to help my life's direction. What should
I capitalize on? What should I avoid? What should I work to
strengthen?

Life Goals – What do I want to accomplish before I die?

Check their alignment with your Mission & Values.
Determine 10-year goals, five-year goals and one-year goals
and check their alignment with your Mission & Values.
Members to share their life plans (30 minutes each).
Members to discuss what they learned from each other.
Members to discuss changes they may make if any.
Determine system for follow through.
Bring this information home, think about it and discuss it
with your significant other.

Goals for Next 12 Months

What goals do I need to achieve in the next 12 months in order to
begin/continue working toward my life goals?

My Life's Mission

My Core Values

SWOT

My Strengths	My Weaknesses
My Opportunities	My Threats

My Life Goals   Deadline

My Goals for Next 12 Months   Deadline

Sample List of Values

Achievement	Knowledge
Excitement	Leadership
Adventure	Love
Community	Loyalty
Family	Nature
Arts	Patience
Creativity	Pleasure
Excellence	Power
Ethics	Recognition
Enlightenment	Relationships
Diplomacy	Religion
Competition	Security
Faith	Responsibility
Gratitude	Status
Forgiveness	Travel
Financial Security	Work
Freedom	
Generosity	
Growth	
Happiness	
Harmony	
Honesty	
Health	
Independence	
Integrity	

Photo Gallery

This exercise requires preparation time at home.

Each member is to determine the 10 most important people in their lives (dead or alive).

Next step is to find a picture of each of the people.

After you've found all the pictures, put them in order starting with the least important.

**Each picture must be on a separate page.
Each member will have 10 minutes at the retreat to share.

The Three-Legged Stool

Each leg of the stool represents a different aspect of life: family, health, work. You assess how much time and energy you currently devote to each aspect in terms of percentages, making sure to add it all up to 100 percent. Once you've finished the assessment, you are ready to tell the group how you hope to change these percentages. Then you can (and should) explain the reason for the gap that exists between what is and what you hope to have and how that gap is currently affecting your life.

This should take 10-15 minutes to prepare and 10-15 minutes to share.

Life Wheel

The wheel encompasses each of the following aspects of life:

Health

Finance

Spirituality

Friends

Family

Intimacy

Work

As you look at the wheel below, rate your life on each item on a scale of 1 to 10, based on how satisfied you are with each. Ten represents very satisfied and one, totally unsatisfied. After you have rated these items, determine which three items you are most dissatisfied with.

Why do you feel that way?

How would you like that to be different?

What, if anything, do you think you are doing to cause this?

What things do you think you can do to change the situation?

Take 15 minutes to prepare and 15 minutes to share with the group.

Exploring Mortality

Take 20 minutes to prepare the response to the following questions:

- When was the last time you feared for your life?

- Do you believe in any sort of an afterlife?

- If somehow you had proof that dispelled that belief, would you live your life differently? How?

- Who do you think would be most affected by your death?

- Whose death would you find most disturbing? Why?

- If you died tomorrow with no opportunity to communicate with anyone, what would you most regret not having communicated?

After you've answered the above questions, please prepare a one-page note to be sent to the one person you identified in the final answer, communicating whatever it is you would regret not having communicated. If no such regret exists, write a letter to be opened by your eldest child on his/her wedding day or graduation day. If you don't have children, write a letter to an important person in your life. This should include some of your most treasured memories with that person.

- Read this note to the group.
- Tell us if you plan on sending it to that person.

Exploring Parents

This exercise requires 30 minutes of preparation during the retreat and about 15 minutes for each person to share.

Members are to write a response to each of the following questions:

Describe your relationship with your mother as a child, as a teen and as an adult.

If your mother is alive, how old is she today and how is her health?

When is the last time you told her you loved her?
When is the last time she said it to you?

Describe your relationship with your father as a child, as a teen and as an adult.

If your father is alive, how old is he and how is his health?

When is the last time you told him that you love him?
When is the last time he said it to you?

Is there anyone else who was an important parent figure in your life? Who? Tell us about him/her.

What have you learned in your relationship with your parents that you will hope to replicate/avoid in your relationship with your children?

Do you think your marriage or significant relationship mirrors your parents? How?

Do you think that your life mirrors your parents? How?

Each member to write a letter to each parent – here are some ideas:

You or a parent dies tomorrow and you have no opportunity to communicate with them.

A parent is already passed away and you write a letter that he/she will read.

You have a regret that you'd like to communicate.

You just want to say, "I love you."

My Favorite Book

Begin this exercise by naming your favorite book of all time, and explain why it is your favorite. If you find it difficult to choose only one book, say that and explain why, but be sure to limit yourself to no more than three. After you've named your favorite(s), list the other books that comprise your list of favorites. As you do so, try to address issues such as:

What element of the books appeal to you: style of writing, characters, genre (fiction, biography, poetry, history, etc.), plot.

What about the book do you remember best? Did you write down any excerpts; if so, what were they?

In what way does the book relate to your life?

What do you know about the author?

Forks

This exercise requires advance preparation.

Think about the critical moments in your life. These are points where a decision you made has affected the course of the rest of your life. These forks in the road may have affected where you lived, worked, went to school and whom you met. Which events have resulted in a change in the course of your life? Were you to make the decision again, would it be the same and why? What do you know now that you didn't know then, and how would that have changed your decision?

Leadership and Self-Deception

Over the years, each of us has developed blindness to problems that we have, to the degree that we actually don't see how we have — or, in some cases, ARE — these problems. The process of discovering these problems is liberating and life-changing, and it makes it possible to repair years of damage in relationships and in behavior.

In preparation for this exercise, read the book, *Leadership and Self-Deception*, by the Arbinger Institute. (Since this requires more advance preparation than normal, more advance warning to the members of the group is imperative.)

After you've read the book, do the following:

Create a list of five boxes that you carry around or five people with whom you are in the box.

Describe each of the boxes above and the self-deception and/or justification you derive from it.

Tell the group what your plan is to get out of each of those boxes, and more specifically, what you plan to do to resolve what you've discovered.

This exercise can take two weeks or more to prepare and up to 60 minutes per person to share.

The Life Walk

This exercise requires advance preparation by the group leader or a volunteer. Take sheets of 8-1/2" x 11" paper and, in large letters indicate five-year periods, starting with 0-5 years, and continuing until the bracket contains the age of the oldest member in the group. (Obviously, the materials can also be prepared using a laser printer.) Once all the sheets have been prepared, they are laminated, since group members will be walking on them.

During the meeting or the retreat, the tiles are laid out so that you can take up to 15 minutes to walk the tiles describing significant events that happened during the ages identified on each one. You describe these events in the present tense, as if they are happening as the story is being told.

The Castle

The Castle is one of the most versatile of the exercises described here, and it can be done with lots of variations. Also, it requires no advance preparation by the members of the group.

Close your eyes, relax and take a couple of deep breaths. If you have any kind of meditative music it is a good idea to use it. When you are ready, your group leader or some other group member will read the following in a soothing voice:

"Imagine that you're walking on your favorite beach. You can smell the ocean. You can hear the waves crashing. Feel the wind brushing your hair and the temperature is perfect. You are very comfortable and relaxed. As you look up into the distance, you see the most beautiful castle. You decide to walk toward the castle and before you know it you are at the door. As you walk in you see several rooms. As you look at the rooms, they each have a label. One is the room of 'great memories.' The next is the room of 'regrets.' Then there's the room of 'sad times.' Then there's the room of 'triumphant events.'

"You decide to walk into the room of 'sad times.' You walk in the room and you make a left turn. On the wall you see pictures of your first five years of life that remind you of these sad times. As you keep walking, you now see pictures of the next five years that remind you of sad times. You keep walking around the room and the pictures are now from your teens, then your twenties, (pause), all the way to the present. As you turn the last corner you see a chair. In the chair there is someone who has caused you great sadness. You decide to forgive this person and you give him/her a hug. Then you continue around the room and on your way out you see a mirror. You look in the mirror and you are reminded of something you have done that has made someone sad and you forgive yourself.

"Then you walk out the door back onto the beach and you keep walking and you find yourself (back at the meeting area). You may open your eyes."

This can be repeated with another room substituting the names of the rooms as appropriate. After each session, you and all the other members of the group will be asked, one at a time, the following questions:

What are three things of significance that you saw on the wall?

Who was in the chair?

What did you think of when you looked in the mirror?

Is there anything else that was significant that you could share with the group?

Unfinished Business

This exercise does not require advance preparation.

There are times in our lives when we have some unfinished business with important people in our lives. Maybe we have not talked to a sibling, a parent, or an offspring in too many years. Maybe we have a bad relationship with someone who has tried to control us, or vice versa.

- What unfinished business do you have?
- How long has it been?
- What happened to start the problem?
- What can you do to resolve it?
- How do you think the other person feels?

Brown Bag Exercise

This exercise does require advance preparation of about one hour at home.

Find 10 objects to represent the 10 most important things in your life. For example, my family was number one, and I had a photograph. My work was represented by a business card, sports by a golf ball, etc. Put the items into a brown paper bag. Then, you and your PEG members will take turns revealing your 10 things. You start with the tenth most important and lead up to the most important. It's important that you go into great detail; you can expect it to take more than three hours for 12 PEG members to participate.

What Makes You Cry?

This exercise requires no advance preparation. There was a time when crying was only for girls. It was not appropriate for boys, let alone men. This served to repress emotions for both men and women, since crying became associated with less than professional, "cool" behavior. The resulting suppression of emotions was unhealthy to say the least. Crying is one of the most cleansing of experiences. Everyone is moved by different things and to varying degrees. Describing those instances – or lack of them – is the point of this exercise. Here is what you talk about:

- Do you cry in movies?
- When was the last time you cried?
- What single event made you cry the most?
- Can you discern a theme enveloping what things make you emotional?

Take about five minutes to go through the questions.

What Drives You?

In preparation for this exercise, read *Man's Search for Meaning* by Victor Frankl. (To give yourself time to really read the book and digest it, it may be important that you and your PEG members have at least one month's notice.)

Prepare responses to the following questions:

1. Describe a time when you felt your life had no meaning.

2. Have your perspectives on life changed in any way as a result of reading the book? How?

3. What was the cause of this feeling?

4. Did you overcome it?

5. Do you feel that your life has meaning today?

6. What are the things in your life that give meaning to your life?

Are any of these things so essential that without them life is not worth living? Which?

IN BRIEF:

Using a proven technique for eliciting candid descriptions of life experiences and descriptions of feelings can smooth the way for more meaningful exchange.

In a PEG setting, it is important to:

- Choose a technique that will include every member.

- Prepare in advance.

- Schedule time and the appropriate methods for closure after the exercise.

CHAPTER TWELVE:
Determining Topics

ver the years there has been an evolution in how groups determine what to talk about.

In most groups, the meeting begins with a session during which everyone does a check-in to update the group on what is new since the last meeting. This is then followed by one or two presentations in which a member has the opportunity to address an issue with which he/she would like some support. The following are the various ways to determine topics:

Wait-and-See Method

One way to determine which member will get to address his/her issue is by waiting to see what is shared during the updates and from there choosing who will get to present that day.

This method has the advantage of being spontaneous but it has some significant disadvantages as well. The main ones include:

The presenter does not have the opportunity to properly prepare by meeting with a coach.

In some cases, no one wants to present, leaving the group wondering what to do.

The more gregarious members will volunteer to present more readily, while those who are less forthcoming (or even the normally easy-going person who is in the middle of a particularly difficult crisis) may not volunteer. Effectively, that can mean that those who could benefit the most are the least likely to come forward.

Group members may suffer by not having had the opportunity to think about the issue in advance, and thereby assure that the support they provide is both well-considered and relevant.

Because of these weaknesses, I typically urge strongly that the Wait and See Method be avoided, with two important exceptions. First, when a member of the group is faced with a crisis situation and asks to have the opportunity to deal with what may well be an emergency basis, that presentation takes precedence, even when another member may have prepared a formal presentation. Second, sometimes during the update portion of the meeting, one individual's update can clearly need extended time immediately. In such a case, the group can decide to continue hearing from that member. His or her update then becomes the topic for that meeting.

In both of these cases, of course, it is important to assure that all group members are comfortable with the change from what had originally been planned.

Random Assignment Method

This method of determining who will present is forthright and simple, but may at the same time be less than optimal. A schedule is simply laid out, assigning dates to various group members. Yes, this assures that there will be a presenter at each meeting because each meeting has a person assigned to present. The disadvantage is that there is no correlation between the need to present and the timing to present.

The Parking Lot Method

In the parking lot method, groups determine a list of member issues. If a group has eight members and each has at least three issues, (one personal, one business, and one family) then there are potentially 24 issues from which to choose. That's at a minimum! I don't know about you, but I usually have about five things on which I can get some input.

Once the group has created this list, each person prioritizes his/her issue based on importance and urgency as follows:

Each person tells the group on a scale of 1-10, 1 being most important, how important the issues he or she has identified are. Once importance is determined, each person assesses in the same way how pressing the issue is – how soon should it be addressed? You express this in the number of days you feel comfortable waiting.

The two numbers are then multiplied, and the person with the lowest number presents first. Consider the following chart:

Name	Issue	*	T	P
John	Potential Divorce	1	7	7
Suzy	Finding New Job	3	30	90

indicates importance; T is the number of days by which the issue must be addressed; P is the group's priority index.

This is a simplified parking lot with only two members and two issues. As you can see, while both John and Suzy have important issues, John assigned a higher level of importance to his issue at a level 1 compared to Suzy's level 3. Likewise John feels that he has less time to address his issue than Suzy does hers. The priority index reflects this since John has a much higher priority (7) as compared to Suzy (90).

The smaller the number on the priority index, the closer that person is to the fire. Successful groups focus on helping members who are closer to the fire versus issues that are of general interest to a majority of the group. Where there's a crisis, there is an opportunity for the group to bond and to make a difference.

The grid (to right) serves two purposes here. First, you can see how it codifies and separates issues. Second, however, you also can see that while this might appear at first to be an objective, dispassionate and discriminating way to choose, it is subject to the judgment of each of the individuals. While Alan's choice of job offers appears to be the issue that should be dealt with first, it would be difficult indeed to judge it more pressing than the substance abuse of a son or a breast cancer scare.

What happens in practice is that after all of the group's issues are congregated into one chart such as this one, when each member sees the other issues on the table, there are often suggested changes. For example, while Alan may have thought his choice was really crucial because of the time pressures, he might well demur to what he sees as more life-bending issues.

Here's the way the index might look for a group of eight.

Name	Issue	*	T	P
Sandra	Breast cancer scare	1	20	20
Hadip	Pending merger	6	120	720
Monique	Age discrimination suit	3	10	30
Jose	Bankruptcy	2	15	30
Marion	New marketing plan	7	40	280
Jim	Suspected substance abuse of son	2	4	8
Susanna	Sale of home, move to new city	6	10	60
Alan	Choosing between two job offers	2	2	4
Robin	Upcoming confrontation with executive committee	3	14	42

Similarly, Sandra, seeing how others have presented their issues, might rethink her choice of 20 days as the time period. You can see her thought process, can't you? The 20 days was how long she had to wait to get a follow-up mammogram, so that's what she put down. But, yes, she couldn't sleep right now, her future and the choices she had to make are today's issues. Maybe the number should have been 1.

In essence, as groups work, they use the parking lot as a tool, but not always as the final word.

IN BRIEF:

Be aware that scheduling presentations requires participation by all members of the group.

Choose the method that you believe will encourage equal participation by all members and assure that the most pressing issues are dealt with expeditiously.

Always recognize that crisis issues, whether they are reported by a member ahead of time or arise as part of an update or presentation, take precedence.

CHAPTER THIRTEEN:
Adding New Members

 dding new members to your group is something you are going to have to do sooner or later. After the initial bonding and building trust, it seems inconceivable to some people that someone new can join the group and get to the same level of comfort as the rest of the members have achieved.

Like it or not, these groups do have attrition, albeit very low in most cases. Members leave groups for a variety of reasons. These reasons may be voluntary or involuntary. For example, members may move away, find it impossible to make the time commitment to the group, or decide that what he or she was looking for in the group is not being provided. And, of course, the group itself may decide to expel the member for lack of commitment or loyalty, or an abrogation of the elements of confidentiality and trust.

When it is time to add new members to your group there are some guidelines that we've found to be helpful:

1. Make sure that everyone has a vote on the new member(s). There's nothing worse than adding a member physically and losing someone mentally. This is not about black-balling; it is about making sure that everyone in the group is comfortable and open.

2. Diversity ensures the richness of the group. Over the years we've seen groups of all women, all men, all one ethnicity, etc. Any way you can diversify within the criteria of the group, the group will benefit. Obviously, the diversification must fit within the agreed-upon mission. For example, a group of CEOs of public companies may prefer not to add the CEO of a private company or a not-for-profit organization, on the premise that they prefer shared professional experiences.

3. A new member is more comfortable when he or she is not the only new kid on the block. In addition, every time a new member is added to the group, there is a certain disruption of the group. Therefore, we've found that it's best to add new members two at a time.

4. After adding new members, it's important to take the time to get to know them and to allow them the time to get to know the group. The optimal time to introduce new members to a group is a short time before the group's annual retreat. Having attended one or two regular meetings, the new member can be assimilated more easily in the more intense, extensive format of the retreat.

5. Prior to accepting new members, it is a good idea to share with them the group's constitution or guidelines and meeting logistics to ensure that they can commit to the group. If the group's schedule is not flexible, there is no reason to add a member only to have to remove him/her for attendance issues within a few months.

IN BRIEF:

Membership turnover is a given, so be prepared to add new members in a way that strengthens your group.

Involve all members in the identification and selection of candidates for membership.

Keep in mind the group constitution and your need for appropriate diversification.

For ease of assimilation of new members, add them two at a time when possible and take all the steps to assure they understand how the group works and can be available for all of the meetings for at least the first six months.

CHAPTER FOURTEEN:
Dealing with Conflict and Removing Members

 ike it or not, conflict will arise. In fact, some would argue that without conflict, a group never becomes real. According to M. Scott Peck in his book, *A Different Drum*, a group of this sort starts out as a "Pseudo Community," where members exchange pleasantries and pretend all is well. During this phase, members have concerns that they do not express. Expressing these issues shifts a group to the next phase, which he calls "Chaos." Here members have strong feelings toward each other, and unless they tell their truth, the group will stay in this phase. Once the members have told their truth the group can shift to the next phase and become "Real Community."

Another shorthand version of this same process used by some group facilitators is "gripe, grope, group." Facing issues squarely and dealing with them skillfully is a precursor for the strongest and best group interaction.

In other words, conflict is not bad. In fact, it's good so long as it is handled properly.

The following are some steps to keep in mind for properly handling conflict:

1. Address the person(s) with whom you have an issue directly. Do not go to a third party.

2. If you have an issue with a member of the group, the problem is yours, at least until you bring it to the attention of that person.

3. Address the behavior that is causing the problem. If I'm not happy with you constantly being tardy, that is something we can work with. If instead I say "I don't like you," that is not something we can work with.

4. Address problems as soon as possible before they fester and blow up.

5. Avoid ultimatums where one member or another has to lose.

6. Clearly express your issues by stating the facts, your judgments, your feelings and what you want. Simply spewing a combination of judgments and feelings is not enough.

7. If you don't agree about the facts, the group leader can be called to mediate.

Still there may be no agreement. If so, involving the entire group is the next course of action.

Conflict is not comfortable or easy for many, but I can tell you from personal experience that it is far better than conflict avoidance.

What must be avoided at all costs is triangulation, which is the situation when two members of the group discuss a third, rather than either of them addressing the third directly. When this begins to occur the cohesion of the group is severely threatened.

IN BRIEF:

When conflict arises, deal with it forthrightly, honestly and without unnecessary delay.

Avoid a win/lose dichotomy.

Adhere carefully to appropriate language protocol, thereby refusing to engage in attacks or harsh judgments. If needed, seek mediation.

Begin first with one-on-one confrontation. If that does not resolve the issue, involve the entire group. At all costs avoid the collusion of two or more members against another.

CHAPTER FIFTEEN:
Group Leadership from Within

O ne of the keys to the success of PEGs is equality. This often presents a challenge for the group leader, who has a critical and delicate role. The leader needs to behave as a member first and a leader second. Yet he/she must be organized and sensitive to member emotions and to group dynamics.

If the leader is autocratic, the members will resent it. If the leader is unorganized, the group will wander. The leader, especially here, must lead by example.

Equally important is that no one member of the group assume a leadership position for too extended a period of time, even if he or she is willing and acting effectively. Leadership rotation refreshes the group processes and solidifies inclusion of all members in it, since each has the opportunity to serve. For most group leaders, a one-year term is just about perfect.

Naturally, there are exceptions. If you are serving as group leader and for whatever reason – some unforeseen pressures from either business or personal perspective – you find it difficult to spend the time and effort necessary to do a good job, it is your responsibility to address that issue with your group, and ask to be replaced. One group had an experience that serves as an excellent example.

Originally composed of 10 members, this group had been together for more than seven years. Two of its members had moved away, and the group had decided to delay finding any new members for a while, content to meet as a smaller number. Ellen had served as group leader the second year they met together, and now had been selected to serve again. Soft-spoken, eminently fair, amazingly adept at finding a way to defuse tense situations, she began her year with eagerness. The first two meetings went well, and she was pleased to see that the smaller group was operating successfully even without the departed members. The first week in March, though, she received a call in the wee hours of the morning. Her mother had had a stroke. After the terror of the initial two weeks, Ellen and her brothers moved their mother into a nursing home an hour and a half away from Ellen's office and two hours away from her home. Thus began what promised to become an extended period of rehabilitation.

Having already missed one meeting and, in her own mind, poorly prepared for the next one, she decided to tell the group that she would like to step down. A difficult, but necessary decision, as she described it to the group. With regret they accepted her suggestion, and together decided that Evan, the only one of them who had not yet served as group leader, should take her place. Well-liked but definitely the quietest of the group members, he accepted the role. It was clear that he was serving out of conscientiousness, not real desire. And the upcoming retreat was going to be a challenge for him. Group exercises were not his forte. In fact, he was what his dad had sometimes called a "doubtful starter."

The retreat started on time and went smoothly for the first day. Then, at breakfast, with no warning, Bryan, one of the more extroverted members, erupted. With equanimity that surprised the entire group – most of all himself – Evan firmly guided the discussion back onto solid ground. Certainly, Ellen might have been just as adroit. What is important to remember, though, is that one of the salient features of successful PEGs is that they create an environment that maximizes the potential of each individual, as well as of the group as a whole.

IN BRIEF:

Every member can be a leader, given the right training and a firm level of commitment. Successful groups:
Train every member to moderate.

Set terms for facilitators/group leaders, typically one year, but never more than two in sequence.

Expect facilitators/group leaders who, for whatever reason, find they cannot commit the time and effort necessary to lead well, to step down, so that another can step in and serve.

CHAPTER SIXTEEN:
Facilitated vs. Volunteer-Run

ome groups decide the issue of a group leader/facilitator by choosing to use a professional instead of assigning the responsibility to one of their number. Deciding whether to use a professional periodically or for every meeting obviously is a matter of preference, and also of cost. While a good facilitator can cost several thousand US dollars (or the equivalent in other currencies), the fact that these professionals are in high demand gives credence to the argument that the fresh, objective insight such a person brings almost invariably strengthens a group.

In addition, some of the organizations that sponsor PEGs for senior business executives offer professionals not only for moderation/ facilitation, but also as consultants and/or executive coaches.

While I obviously know and appreciate the value of professional facilitation, since that is part of my own business, the strongest groups with whom I have worked (assuming they meet weekly or monthly) are those who use a professional at least once a year, and optimally two times — either at one retreat and one regular meeting or at two retreats. PEGs who use volunteer leadership also regularly train all of their members (another part of what I do). While the training sessions are intended to improve the leadership ability of all members, another no less important result is that in the process the group as a whole coheres.

Perhaps the most important time to include professional advice for any group is during the formation process. Another instance when professionals can be engaged is for remedial work. This occurs most often in two situations: when conflict threatens the stability of the group or when the group is faltering and needs revitalization. In both of these instances, group members may well be too close to the problem to be able to find the equanimity and objectivity necessary to find a solution. A skilled professional facilitator has a much better chance at success.

When a group meets only quarterly or even less frequently, my experience indicates a professional facilitator is almost a necessity. The time elapsed between meetings can undermine group cohesion and the number of issues that may need to be addressed can be daunting.

Professionals familiar with PEG dynamics can help immensely.

Finally, a word on how to select a facilitator. I cannot reiterate too often that a PEG is not a support group in the traditional sense. Still, when the group functions at the highest levels (see the next chapter) and is dealing with issues of grave importance to one or more members, the meetings can become highly charged and need skillful moderation. Since there are a number of very fine meeting facilitators who may have little or no understanding of how PEGs work, it is crucial that the group choose an individual who has proven experience in group process and most important, understands that the group's confidentiality understanding must be honored and, reciprocally, the group will honor his/hers.

Here, then, are some guidelines to follow in selecting and contracting with an outside group leader/facilitator.

Assure the individual has both training and experience. Advanced degrees alone are not enough. Nor is a decade acting as chairman of an executive committee. Facilitation is a skill that is part craft — meaning it can be taught — and part art — meaning it requires talent. You want both artist and craftsperson, and it might well be hard to make sure you're getting that ahead of time. Do your homework! One of the best ways to find someone who knows and operates with PEG protocols and procedures is to get recommendations from other PEGs who have hired such professionals.

Create as much common ground as possible. For example, while I consider myself fully capable of facilitating a PEG of female entrepreneurs, I most likely would assign one of my female colleagues instead, on the premise that the more shared the history, the faster the ability to reach optimal performance.

Cover all of the bases on the contractual arrangement. For example, what happens if the facilitator is unable to make a meeting? Can an alternate from the same contract firm step in?

Or, should you as a group find it necessary to cancel a meeting altogether, does the facilitator who has set aside the time to work with you still get his/her fee? Be sure to address confidentiality fully in the contract.

Specify the responsibility of the facilitator for (1) logistical arrangements; and (2) assigned tasks between meetings. Most groups are disinclined to pay the rates of a professional facilitator for the time to find and arrange for meeting space, etc., but it's not unheard of. Similarly, the group needs to determine at the outset whether it has any financial responsibility for facilitator follow-up with individual members between meetings. Similarly, what if a member wishes to hire the facilitator for other, non-PEG related work? Are there any perceived conflicts of interest in the resulting consultant/client relationship?

Specify a means of terminating the contract. Good facilitators are busy people. From their point of view, setting aside time for your contract keeps them from selling their services during that same time for another group. So working on a month-to-month basis is most often not acceptable. Still, if for whatever reason the facilitator's work is not what the PEG expects, a means of termination needs to be specified in advance.

IN BRIEF:

When you are deciding on whether and when to use a professional facilitator, it is important to engage in the necessary research and preparation to assure your selection is not just workable, but optimum.

Make your choice and contract for the services you need with careful attention to your needs as a group.

Don't forget confidentiality!

CHAPTER SEVENTEEN:

Levels of Group Development

O ver time a group will reach different levels of comfort, trust and emotional involvement. Conversations will become more meaningful and the experience much more rewarding. Unfortunately, this rarely happens quickly nor does it happen without some work.

Level I

In Level I, members exchange pleasantries and share little that actually requires confidentiality. Members are still uncomfortable and therefore do not share issues that are risky. Issues they do present may well have been discussed with many people outside the group. Level I issues are likely to be professionally oriented, and the presenter (see Chapter 21) very likely believes he or she already has the answer to this issue.

Level II

During Level II, members begin discussing issues of greater sensitivity. These are issues that they have discussed but only with a select few. This is a sensitive matter. The presenter has clearly shown vulnerability and he/she does not already have the answer. The issue can be challenging with no simple solution.

Level III

At Level III a member will bring something to the group that he/she has never discussed with anyone. This issue will always be of a personal nature, and it will be emotional for at least one person.

Level IV

Level IV occurs as a result of the group discussing an issue that causes an emotional reaction by at least 50 percent of the members of the group. This frequently happens as a result of a traumatic event or a shared meaningful personal issue. Reaching Level IV provides a level of bonding and cohesion that is for many better than what they have achieved with their families.

Reaching higher levels of group development requires time and hard work. The hard work includes member commitment, strict adherence to confidentiality and the use of appropriate language. In Chapters 7 and 9, I've discussed the confidentiality and language protocol issues, and I've touched throughout this book on the need for member commitment. Still, it's worth a bit of additional exploration here.

Higher levels of group development are simply out of reach unless meetings of the full group are the rule. By far the vast majority of successful groups incorporate into their constitution the means of assuring that attendance at meetings takes precedence in members' planning.

As you noted from the sample constitutions presented on pages 46 through 53, some groups are more rule-bound than others, using a point system to measure tardiness and non-attendance. Others simply say that if a member begins to miss too many of the meetings to grow with the group, he or she should resign. Whatever the mechanism to create it, consistent attendance is crucial. A subtler but no less important point is that attendance means more than bodily presence. Members who can't stay out of communication with the outside world for the length of the meeting aren't really in attendance. Cell phones and PDAs are not appropriate appurtenances in PEG meetings. Yes, there can be exceptions if there is a crisis afoot or an important deadline. Most highly functioning groups require, though, that the exception be explained and accepted by the group as a whole.

IN BRIEF:

Groups operate on different levels of engagement. Those that mature and provide the richest experience for their members are able to reach the deeper levels of interchange at least periodically.

Achieving these deeper levels requires openness, honesty, effort and ongoing commitment on the part of every member.

Regular attendance and commitment of not only time, but full attention on the part of every member are crucial elements.

CHAPTER EIGHTEEN:

Inter-Meeting Communication

Inter-meeting communication is necessary from an administrative perspective, but it is not necessary for group effectiveness. Particularly when PEGs are sponsored by an umbrella organization or have members who participate in the same profession or live in the same geographic area, it is a natural consequence that some of the members will have social interaction. The important point to remember is that it is natural and not created artificially. I have both been a member of and counseled groups who have attempted to force some form of systematic interaction between meetings. They met with no success. Sound relationships are not created by force.

Successful PEG group meetings by their very nature require time and commitment at a level that may be creating pressure for members as it is. Any additional time or effort can become a challenge for some. In addition, some members will be naturally drawn to some, but not necessarily to all of their PEG colleagues.

Is there a problem if small groups of members become especially friendly? Well, only if they abrogate the confidentiality agreement. Two members discussing the issue or personality of other members outside the confines of the PEG meeting can eventually undermine group cohesion, unless they are particularly careful to respect confidentiality and also to bring to the entire group any issues they among themselves identify.

IN BRIEF:

Communication and socializing among members between meetings is neither encouraged nor discouraged by the PEG. Instead, it is a function of the preferences and experiences of individual members.

The issue to be addressed is the maintenance of appropriate confidentiality of any issues that arise within the PEG setting.

CHAPTER NINETEEN:
Evaluating Group Performance

valuating group performance is an important part of ensuring that the group is meeting member needs. While it is encouraged that members speak up when they have an issue, often constructive criticism does not come without prompting.

One trait of successful groups is their having established a culture within which each member takes responsibility for his/her own experience. This serves as each member's own self-check for how he/she is feeling about the group. There are two effective ways to encourage members to take such responsibility:

1. A member says: "Time out, I have an issue with ...." specifying a behavior within the group with which he/she is not happy.

2. A member who realizes that the group discussions have become less than effective—superficial, overly confrontational, dominated by a subset of members rather than equally inclusive, etc. — takes the risk of sharing his assessment and asks the group to either agree or challenge his view and take action accordingly.

In addition to relying on members to take responsibility for personal group assessment, it is also possible to measure group performance in a more formal fashion as part of the meeting agenda. At the end of each meeting, the group leader systematically asks each member to take a minute to share what he or she liked and disliked about the meeting. This not only assures that all members' opinions are heard (instead of only those who feel prompted to share their feelings), but it gives the group an opportunity to adjust in subsequent meetings.

Finally, it is highly recommended that groups measure their performance using a member survey every six to 12 months. Below is a typical survey instrument:

Please rate each of the following on a scale of 1-10 (10 being best):

___ **Attendance**

___ **Tardiness**

___ **Group Leader Preparation**

___ **Group Leader Ability to Facilitate Meeting**

___ **Openness of Members**

___ **Presentation Selection**

___ **Depth of Presentations**

___ **Presenter Preparation**

___ **Coaching**

___ **Language Protocol**

___ **Conflict Resolution**

___ **Timing**

___ **Retreats**

After each member has completed the survey, the group leader compiles the results for discussion with the group, an excellent opportunity to address all relevant issues at one time and make appropriate adjustments. A particularly good time to conduct this survey is before a retreat, since there is often the opportunity during the retreat agenda to deal with administrative issues in a more comprehensive way than might be possible at a normal meeting.

IN BRIEF:

PEG members take responsibility for their own experience, and find constructive ways to address troublesome issues/ situations that may diminish the value they receive.

Group leaders assure that: (1) at the end of each meeting there is a process through which every member can evaluate that session; and (2) at least twice a year a member survey is completed, with the results compiled and distributed to every member.

CHAPTER TWENTY:

Rejuvenating Your Group – Retreats

 single retreat is said to have as much value for group growth as six to 12 months of meetings – reason enough for groups to schedule at least one and optimally two retreats each year.

What is a retreat? A retreat is an organized, two-day, out of town meeting that provides a group with the opportunity to rebuild, rejuvenate and grow. A successful retreat is planned using a work component and a play component.

The work component includes a formal agenda with updates, presentations, exercises (see Chapter 11) and housekeeping.

The play component can be anything from skiing to rock climbing to white water rafting to any number of parlor games. And, of course, shared meals are an important element.

Retreats can be held at a variety of locations: hotels, bed and breakfasts, resorts, private vacation homes, even boats. From my experience, vacation homes can be particularly effective retreat sites, because the group can stay together in a family atmosphere, enjoy total privacy and share some of the menial tasks, such as cooking, that engender a stronger sense of friendship.

A key consideration in planning retreats is funding. Because retreat attendance is mandatory, it is critical that the retreat does not require more money than even one member can afford. Obviously, this may create an uncomfortable discussion for a new group. If there is concern that one or more members may have some financial concerns, it is good to ask each person to take a scrap piece of paper and write on it how much he/she is willing to spend, anonymously, of course. All the papers are passed to the group leader who announces the budget per person based upon the lowest amount.

Similarly, members may have differing flexibility in terms of time, so it is important that the travel time to the retreat site be such that no one member finds it too much for his or her schedule.

Simply put, the group should do whatever is necessary to assure that every member can comfortably attend.

The retreat provides an opportunity for the members to self discover as well as to get better acquainted with their fellow members, especially new ones. It is not at all unusual for new group members to feel some hesitancy before attending the first retreat. Seasoned groups, though, quickly realize the value of the retreat and look forward to the intensity of the experience.

IN BRIEF:

Retreats have significant, measurable value for PEGs.

Two per year is an ideal number, but at least one per year is necessary.

Retreats should be carefully planned in advance for a time and place that will assure complete and convenient attendance for all members.

Sample Retreat Agenda

Sunday

6:00pm	Working Dinner
	Confidentiality Reminder
	Introductions
	Expectations
	Review of Mission Statement
6:30pm	Gestalt Language Protocol
	The Forum Experience
	Levels of Forum Development
7:00pm	The Ungame
7:30pm	Exploring Marriage
9:30pm	The Parking Lot
9:45pm	Presentation #1
11:00pm	Cigars

Monday

7:00am	Breakfast
7:30am	Morning Walk
8:00am	Walk Review
8:15am	Presentation #2
10:00am	Survey Results
10:45am	Review Constitution
12:00pm	Xualization
	Program Evaluation
12:30pm	Lunch

CHAPTER TWENTY-ONE:
The Roles of the Members

 fter years of working with PEGs, my colleagues and I determined that it is really important that as many members as possible are involved in group processes.

Member

Members without a designated assignment other than attendance actually have as important a role to play as those with additional responsibilities. Indeed, playing the role of the member comes first and foremost. A member who overlooks this role for the stated purpose of any of the following roles is doing the group a disservice.

The role of the member requires physical, mental and emotional commitment. At each meeting, the member is asked to follow the group's rules including attendance, punctuality, confidentiality and the Gestalt Language Protocol. At least once each year, a member becomes the presenter. Yes, there are times when a member may feel he or she has little need to bring an issue forward, but it is important to remember that a member who never presents creates a concern among other members. And, of course, at every meeting it is the responsibility of each member to be honest and forthcoming with any concerns about the group or other members of the group.

Group Leader

The role of the group leader is to facilitate the meetings. This includes, but is not necessarily limited to:

- Providing a written agenda, either before the meeting or at the beginning.

- Assuring that each of the other roles below has been assigned to a member.

- Leading the group through the process of determining future presenters, coaches and meetings.

- Taking the pulse of the group at least once per year to ascertain any potential problems or concerns or appropriate adjustments.

- Ensuring that the group holds a retreat at least once per year.

The group leader's term is typically one year. Some groups prefer to provide for the group leader to be elected for a second term if the group is unanimously agreed, but few if any use a group leader for an extended number of years. In fact, when a group uses the same group leader for a period of years, there is an excellent chance that, no matter how skillful the group leader may be, there is a dangerous lack of group dynamism and of continuing commitment among the other members.

Presenter

The presenter's role is best described very simply – be prepared. That preparation includes:

- Meeting with a coach prior to the meeting in which he/she will be presenting.

- Clearly articulating to the coach what he/she hopes to get from the presentation.

- Identifying the most important thing that the group is to focus on.

- Providing well-organized information for the group, in sufficient detail that the meeting can be effective for all involved. That information most normally should include:

  - **Background** – what is the relevant history?

  - **Current situation** – what is taking place now that has caused the issue to bubble up?

  - **Options** – what options have been considered?

  - **Future implications** – what are the implications to the options?

In addition, the presenter may bring collateral material, spreadsheets or whatever else will be valuable. Some material can even be sent in advance so long as confidentiality is ensured.

Coach

The role of the coach is to meet with the presenter prior to the meeting during which the presentation is scheduled. This meeting can last up to 30 minutes and is best done in person. The coach's job is to:

- Help the presenter identify the objective of the presentation.

- Identify the presenter's point(s) of vulnerability.

- Design a warm-up question that will help the members of the group identify with the presenter emotionally before he/she presents.

The coach can be chosen by the member or by the group leader. Some groups have the presenter at one meeting become the coach for the next meeting. While there are a few groups who name one coach for an entire year, that is in my experience by far the weakest method. Just as they do with a perpetual group leader, group dynamics suffer with the use of one coach over an extended number of meetings.

With the recent growth of all kinds of coaches – personal trainers, diet/nutrition coaches, life coaches, executive coaches – it is important to spend a little time here defining very specifically why there is a coach at all. PEGs often find that they struggle to determine just what he or she wants from the presentation. For example, let's assume the presenter is discussing his need to dissolve a business partnership. He will likely give the group the history of the partnership, how long it has been in existence, how it has evolved over time and why he now thinks it should be terminated. Without appropriate coaching, the group may believe he wants to hear their experiences on the best ways to go about such a dissolution, when what he is really after is deciding, once the partnership is dissolved, whether he should look for another partner or go it alone. Those are the experiences he wants to hear about.

How does the coach do the work? I have provided some sample coaching worksheets to illustrate the process. Ideally, presenter and coach meet in person about two weeks before the presentation, and spend enough time to clarify the relevant issues, especially the purpose and focus of the presentation. In using the worksheet, the coach might well ask:

TOPIC: Is your topic principally business, personal or family related? If you consider it a mixture, which do you want to concentrate on?

PURPOSE: What is the one thing you'd like to get from the group? This is a pretty complicated issue and you could choose to present on three or four different things. Which piece of this situation is the largest or the one that keeps you up at night? Be specific, now. Asking for help with your problem or how to make a tough decision is too generic for the group to be able to share relevant experience.

BOUNDARIES: Is there anything within your control that you've decided for or against that you don't want us to discuss?
OBSTACLES: Is there something that's outside of your control that gets in your way of achieving your purpose?

FEELINGS: Sad, mad, glad, ashamed and afraid are the five core emotions. Which of those resonate(s) with you?

CAUSE FOR FEELINGS: What is it that you're afraid of?

COMMUNICATION STARTER: The communication starter is a question that we will ask the members to answer before you present. It's not intended to answer your purpose; instead, it's intended to get the members in your shoes and to let you know that you're not alone in your feelings and vulnerabilities. Tell me if the following question would serve that purpose. Tell us about a time that you were afraid for the future of your company because two key players were not getting along.

Caution: The role of the presentation coach is NOT to solve the presenter's problem, or control the presenter's purpose. In fact, the coach needs to be careful NOT to listen to the presenter's entire story.

At the beginning of the presentation, the coach asks the members to answer the communication starter. He/she helps assure that the members do not offer solutions, but simply respond to the question itself. Then he explains briefly the topic, purpose, boundaries, obstacles and feelings as he has learned them in the meeting and ensures that members remain within the boundaries as they question the presenter.

Presentation Coaching

Coaching Worksheet

Topic	Business, Personal, Family
Purpose	I'd like the group's experience with...
Boundaries	I don't want to get into....
Obstacles	Things that get in the way are....
Feelings	Sad, Mad, Glad, Ashamed, Afraid
Cause for feelings	
Communication Starter	Tell us about a time that you were (insert feeling from above) (take the cause for the feeling and make up the rest of the question).

Glossary of Terms

Topic	**Business, Personal, Family**
	(identify all that apply)
Purpose	This is the central question that the presenter will present. The process works best when it's focused on only one issue.
Boundaries	Areas that the presenter does not want to discuss either because the presenter has already decided against them or because they can easily take the group on a tangent.
Obstacles	These are things that are outside of the presenter's control that prevent him/her from achieving the purpose.
Feelings	These are the emotions that this issue evokes for the presenter.
Cause for feelings	What creates these feelings for the presenter?
Communication Starter	This is a question that is answered by the members prior to the presenter presenting.

Coaching Worksheet (Example)

<u>Topic</u>	<u>Business, Family</u>
Purpose	Sam would like the group's experience to help him determine how to deal with two family members in the business who do not get along.
Boundaries	He won't fire his brother-in-law as it would create lots of hard feelings with his wife.
Obstacles	He cannot fire his sister because she owns 51% of the company.
Feelings	Afraid
Cause for feelings	The future of the company is at risk because key player are not getting along.
Communication Starter	Tell us about a time that you were afraid for the future of your company `because two key players were not getting along.

Process Police

The role of the process police is to ensure that the group is following the appropriate language protocol. This is done by on-the-spot reminders when the protocol is violated or about to be violated. The member playing this role also changes every meeting.

Timekeeper

The timekeeper has a very important role. Without a timekeeper, some members can dominate the conversation, while others are denied the opportunity to speak enough or at all. The timekeeper simply gives warnings as determined by the group. Usually these warnings are given at the 5 minute mark, 1 minute mark and when time is up as predefined for given sections of the meeting. The timekeeper is designated at the beginning of each meeting.

Note Taker

The note taker simply takes notes on the experiences shared and valuable points. These notes are then given to the presenter at the end of the presentation. The note taker is also designated at the beginning of each meeting. Sometimes it also is the note taker's role to gather any materials at the end of the meeting and make sure they are either destroyed or returned to the presenter. If the note taker is not assigned this responsibility, the group leader and/ or presenter become responsible.

Financial Chair

Each group makes its own determination as to whether or not members will pay dues up front or as they go. If the group does collect dues in advance, a finance chair is chosen to manage the group's funds. This person typically serves a one-year term. It also is important to clarify in advance what individual has authority to sign contracts that obligate the PEG or its sponsoring organization financially. If that is not the responsibility of the financial chair, it is important that he/she be kept informed of any contracts, payment amounts and dates.

Logistics Coordinator

The logistics coordinator is responsible for keeping track of group logistics, and of member attendance/punctuality. He/she also sends meeting directions and reminders as needed. This is a one-year term.

NOTE: All of the above roles are filled by a member of the group and never by an outsider. This is critical for preservation of confidentiality.

IN BRIEF:

No matter what role a PEG member assumes, his or her participation is an important component of every meeting. Understanding the appropriate preparation and procedures for each role and following through with focus and precision creates the foundation for successful meetings, and ultimately group cohesion.

CHAPTER TWENTY-TWO:
Financial Matters

inancial operations are decided by each group, based on consensus among the members. However, there are some things to keep in mind in order to ensure a smooth operation.

It is critical to take all members into account when making financial decisions. Not uncommonly, new members and new groups can be somewhat uncomfortable discussing finances. It is a shame to lose a good member before a retreat (or anytime for that matter) because he/she is unable to pay to have the retreat at The Ritz when the group could have gone to a member's beach house for much less money. For that reason, establishing clear parameters by involving everyone in the group is priority number one.

As suggested earlier, one tip for handling this delicate issue is to ask each person to anonymously write down how much they are willing to spend on dues or on the retreat. The group leader then collects every member's vote and the minimum number is the budget per person.

While it's not absolutely necessary to collect dues up front, doing so certainly makes for easier decision making and at the same time ensures a commitment level on the part of the members.

Depending on when the group meets, it may be that expenses are incurred that require both payments and financial recordkeeping – e.g., a meal is involved, a meeting room rental is required or the group is hiring a professional facilitator. Having a financial officer makes handling these situations efficient and keeps them from absorbing valuable group time and attention.

Many groups operate without a finance chair and with minimal expense. Meeting at member homes or offices can reduce the costs to almost nothing. Still, the group needs to be clear on who is responsible and how money that is collected will be allocated. Within that responsibility, as indicated earlier, is clear delineation of who has the authority to sign contracts that incur financial obligations for the group.

IN BRIEF:

PEGs require clear, upfront decision making on financial issues.

The priority is the comfort of every member in terms of financial commitments. Clear delineation of responsibility for contracting and recordkeeping is also important.

CHAPTER TWENTY-THREE:

Meeting Locations

 s just mentioned, meetings can be held at offices and homes. They can also be held at hotels, conference centers, country clubs and even restaurants provided the location meets the following criteria:

- Accessible and fair to all members
- Quiet
- Soundproof to ensure confidentiality
- Free of interruptions
- Free of ringing telephones
- Comfortable seating
- Properly lit
- Temperature should be cool enough to keep people awake (Those who get cold easily can bring a jacket.)

In our experience, it has been quite valuable to visit member offices at least in the beginning. This is a fascinating way to learn about each other's businesses and work environments. Obviously, this may be either impossible or impractical, but it is recommended otherwise. It is important to note, however, that the host member should make sure his colleagues and staff are informed that the meeting is private and not to be interrupted.

If you will be using a hotel or other formal meeting space requiring a contract, it is important that you specify in writing the group's needs to the staff. For example, many groups include in their letters of agreement the following:

- The room is to be completely set up per our schematic at least 30 minutes before the meeting begins.

- Since our proceedings are confidential, we request that no service personnel interrupt the meeting for refreshing water, etc. Therefore, please assure that all service items have been set to last the duration of the meeting.

- It is our policy not to interrupt meetings for telephone calls, except in the case of emergency. Please instruct your staff accordingly.

IN BRIEF:

Choose meeting space that works best for the most members.

Consider, especially when the group is first formed, using meeting rooms within the office suites of members.

Specify ahead of time the special needs of the group for both comfort and privacy

CHAPTER TWENTY-FOUR:
What to Avoid

 hile there are many things required to make PEGs work effectively, there are many more that can cause them to work ineffectively. Here they are in no particular order:

The Temptation to Violate the Language Protocol

Because this is such a difficult concept to grasp and also because it is so unlike how most of us have learned to communicate over the years, it is a tempting concept to violate. A member may even ask for advice, making it seem not only natural but supportive to provide it. It is important to remember, though, that falling into this trap will only damage the safe environment, the value derived and the group as a whole.

Holding onto Members

Let's face it: there is a lot of commitment required in order for these groups to succeed and for some people that commitment is simply too much or they are just at a point in life where they are unable to commit. Our experience is that unless every member is committed, the value proposition deteriorates. Ultimately, if there's no value, there's no compelling reason to make the commitment. Simply put, without the commitment of each member and without the group enforcing the need for that commitment, PEGs cannot work. One of the biggest mistakes a group can make is holding onto members who are not committed to the group.

Not Rocking the Boat

This does not mean that rocking the boat for the sake of rocking the boat is a good thing. Instead, there may come a time when members develop a comfort level that they have not felt in a long time. Concerned about losing that comfort, they fail to bring forth the things they may be unhappy with. This is a sure-fire way to build a time-bomb that will explode some day.

Sticking with an Ineffective Group Leader

A group leader who is not doing a good job for the group can lead to a quick drop in quality. Moderating is a special form of leading, and it can be jeopardized by any number of things: faltering commitment to the group, disorganization, or failure to participate as a member, to name a few. The corrective course is not necessarily removing the group leader. He/she may be able to correct a given behavior, if it is identified by the group. If not, then it may be time for someone else to step in. Dealing with this issue may best be handled with an outside facilitator, if the group is uncomfortable with the process.

Canceling Meetings

Having regular meetings is a source of comfort and continuity for many members, and at the same time an important source of stability for the group. Granted, it is often difficult to schedule meetings that are convenient for all members. Still, simply canceling is not a good solution, particularly if it is recommended by a member to avoid an absence on his/her record. While there will be unforeseen conflicts, the process of scheduling meetings several months in advance can significantly reduce the conflicts.

Adding New Members without Unanimous Consent

The group is only as good as the cohesion of its members. Adding a new member without unanimous consent makes the member who has not consented feel unrecognized at best, and rejected at worst. While the confidentiality of the group should make all members feel comfortable in explaining their position on the issue, it is possible that a member wishes not to reveal the experience he/she has had with the prospective member. It is, therefore, simply better to require unanimity, without challenge or explanation.

Indirect Discussions

Speaking about a fellow member in his/her absence with another member or non-member can be very dangerous particularly if it is regarding a complaint or a judgment about that person or if it may lead to a breach of confidentiality if overheard. It is for this reason that outside-the-group social interaction should be kept as separate as possible from the PEG meeting agendas and issues.

Attempting to Solve Other Member Problems

The purpose of the group is not to "fix" someone or a situation and it is up to the person with the issue to solve his/her own problem. This is one of the key tenets of these groups. Certainly, the close relationships that can be established in a healthy PEG make the temptation to jump in and "help" a strong one, but it cannot be stressed enough that the strength of the PEG model is that it is neither a therapy group nor a support group in the sense that the latter is usually perceived.

Missing a Retreat

As mentioned earlier, retreats are critical to the growth of these groups. Missing a retreat is typically not allowed, but there may be situations where the group makes an exception for a given member. From that member's perspective, missing the retreat is a tremendous loss, and it is also a loss for the entire group.

Business Dealing

Business dealings among members have a potential for degrading the safety of the environment and the value of the group. It is easy to see that members who engage in a business project are operating under a strong incentive to show the good and not the bad of their side of the deal, which quickly devolves into being dishonest with the group. Obviously if a member owns a coffee shop, simply purchasing a coffee at his/her shop does not constitute a business dealing. Substantial financial commitments, however, can spell trouble.

Sexual Relations

Sexual relations between members obviously are also not healthy for a group, because they almost always create tensions that give birth to discomfort and curtail openness.

IN BRIEF:

Knowing what to avoid is just as important as knowing what to do in creating a successful PEG. Pay attention to the potential for problems and address these issues as early as possible.

CHAPTER TWENTY-FIVE:
Support Groups Within Companies

raditionally support groups have formally existed only outside companies but informally they've existed in companies for years. Unfortunately they've existed in a form that has been "us against them," workers against management. Still, these informal groups have not followed any guidelines and thus provide little value to the company. And, of course, these are in no way PEGs as we are using the term here.

Were support groups within companies to be replaced by – or even trained to be – PEGs, they could provide a tremendous amount of value to the company and to the individual members.

As more and more corporations recognize the validity and effectiveness of executive coaching, it is possible they will also see the value of incorporating the PEG process into either human resources programming or management training, or both.

At this writing, however, there are only a very few such groups operating. Much more common are the groups within trade and professional associations, but even there the PEG process is concentrated frequently in the senior management arena. While there is no doubt that PEGs have worked well and are multiplying rapidly among chief executives, entrepreneurs and others with significant decision making powers in the business world, their wider application could create added value, not only for those employed on other levels, but for the companies as a whole.

IN BRIEF:

While they have been in operation for several decades, until now PEGs have been concentrated in community groups, trade associations, professional societies and on the senior management levels of corporations. Extension of the experience on other levels of employment has great potential.

CHAPTER TWENTY-SIX:

Conclusion

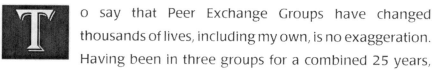 o say that Peer Exchange Groups have changed thousands of lives, including my own, is no exaggeration. Having been in three groups for a combined 25 years, I cannot imagine not having had such a great group of supporters and confidants that I can count on. In my darkest times, they showed me that it's okay. When I thought my world was crashing down, they showed me the light at the end of the tunnel. And when I was feeling down, they showed me that I'm not alone. But most of all, when I was on a runaway train, they pointed to my rescue helicopter that allowed me not just to exit the train but to soar higher than I had ever imagined. To all my Forum members, I thank you all from the bottom of my heart.

Studies have shown that people who live the longest are those with many meaningful relationships in their lives. The second group are those who have lots of acquaintances. The last group are those whose only relationships are their families.

Psychology has told us that people who have an outlet where they can share their challenges and unburden themselves are happier than those who don't. My Forums have provided me with more meaningful relationships than any man deserves and to say that I've had an outlet to unburden myself is an understatement. My wish for every human being is to be in a functional peer exchange group where they can have meaningful, non-judgmental relationships and a true safe environment where they can unburden themselves and grow – life is too short!

CPSIA information can be obtained
at www.ICGtesting.com
Printed in the USA
LVOW08*1210160217
524489LV00015B/261/P